THE STREETWISE GUIDE TO
RENOVATING
YOUR
HOME

About the Author

Since her first house purchase several years ago Alison Cork has renovated property in her spare time for herself, family and friends, tackling everything from flats and town houses to bungalows and country cottages. Educated in Classical art and architecture at Cambridge University, she has developed both a practical and academic interest in buildings, interior decoration and conservation. She divides her spare time between homes in South Wales and London, where she is director of a publishing company.

THE STREETWISE GUIDE TO
RENOVATING YOUR HOME

ALISON CORK

PIATKUS

For Christopher

Acknowledgements

Jim Berry and Morrish & Partners, Patricia Bessey, John Brandenburger, Martin Branston, British Gas plc, British Telecommunications plc, Bernard Broderick and Barclays Bank plc, Martin Burgess, Ernest Cantle OBE and the National Home Improvement Council Educational Trust, Gordon Chard, The Cheltenham and Gloucester Building Society, Tony and Victoria Cork, S. J. Corson and Sons, Paul Errington and Penn Contracting Ltd, Carol Gannon Associates, The Halifax Building Society, Alan Hughes and the BEC, Martin Hulse, The Institute of Electrical Engineers, Jerrum Falkus, Nicholas Jones and the RIBA Bookshop, Ron Lavers, London Electricity plc, Monmouth Borough Council, National Westminster Bank plc, Lester Stump, Dave Swanson, Thames Water Utilities, Christopher Tracy, Webber Brothers Ltd, Westminster City Council. Special thanks to Nick Jackson for his seemingly inexhaustible supply of patience and advice!

The author and publishers would like to thank the following people and organisations for kindly allowing them to reproduce their copyright documents, plans and diagrams in this book:

Figure 3, RIBA Publications; figure 4, BIAT; figures 5 and 22, Penn Contracting Ltd; figures 7 and 13, Westminster City Council Planning and Building Regulations Departments; figures 8, 9 and 12, Jim Berry; figures 10 and 11, Monmouth Borough Council Planning and Building Regulations Departments; figure 14, The Institute of Electrical Engineers; figures 15–21, Dick Vine.

First published in 1995 by
Judy Piatkus (Publishers) Ltd
5 Windmill Street, London W1P 1HF

The moral right of the author has been asserted
A catalogue record for this book is available from the British Library

ISBN 0 7499 1445 9

Designed by Paul Saunders

Typeset by Datix International Limited, Bungay, Suffolk
Printed and bound in Great Britain by
Mackays of Chatham PLC

Contents

Introduction

Enthusiastic as I am about crumbling buildings, even I have to admit that not many people renovate property for the sheer fun of it. Most of you will do so only once or twice in your lives and out of necessity. Furthermore, the vast majority of you will decide that employing a surveyor or architect to handle all the proceedings on your behalf is an unaffordable luxury – which just leaves you to find, instruct and manage the builder. Whether it's the whole house or just the kitchen, it's a prospect which fills the average mortal with dread and has even been known to precipitate a divorce or two. So just why do builders and renovation work cause so much grief?

Well, from the start the odds appear to be stacked against the poor home owner and the entire building industry seems intent on making your life a misery. From your point of view it's really very simple. All you want is a builder who can work to budget, within deadlines and to your specification (and who doesn't walk all over your clean carpets). Not much to ask, is it? The only trouble is that you've never heard of a builder who can do all these things and your friends' tales of woe only serve to confirm your suspicions. You are entering Wild West territory and the cowboys are waiting.

Ask a builder what it is like to work for the average client and he will paint a very different picture. Many customers have unrealistic expectations of what can be achieved within their budget and time frame. They refuse expert advice, make impractical requests, expect little 'extras' to be done for free, change their minds every other day and then consider themselves gypped when the job costs more and takes longer. So just who is at fault and can the problem be avoided?

There is no doubt that bad builders exist and in an industry where there are no formal qualifications required for entry, this state of affairs is hardly surprising and unlikely to improve. Having said that, many of the problems which crop up in property renovations occur as a result of the client's ignorance. Most people are ill prepared for their role; they haven't thought through exactly what it is they want, can hope to achieve or have available to spend. They don't have even the most elementary knowledge of building terms or of their own property, so even if they do find a good builder they can't effectively communicate what it is they want or exercise any real control over the renovation process. Little wonder then that so many renovations end in disappointment, bad feeling and sometimes tears.

My own first home renovation was a real baptism of fire – a Welsh cottage with no modern conveniences and which eventually had everything but its four walls replaced. Add to that recipe a couple of innocents abroad and you will understand why the end result was a triumph of hope over adversity and one of life's minor miracles. But I soon realised that with some basic advice it needn't have been that way and now, several renovations later, I reckon I can smell a dodgy builder a mile off, hold my own in a 'building conversation' and generally get the job done to my satisfaction.

The Streetwise Guide To Renovating Your Home is the result both of these experiences and of countless conversations with builders (both good ones and bad). It aims to spare you the misery and expense of the learning curve and take you through all the stages necessary to achieve a successful property renovation – everything from preparing your brief and finding the right builder for the job to seeing the work finished on time and within budget. Its spells out when you might need professional help other than that of the builder, and how to find your way through the maze of official permissions. It tells you exactly what does lurk under the floorboards and lays out clearly the order in which renovation works should be carried out. It even gives you special tips on how to spot good and bad workmanship – as well as some of the little tricks that builders can get up to. And the advice holds good whatever the size and complexity of the job – be it converting a barn, restoring a period property or repairing a 1960s' bungalow.

A word of caution: you are not in competition with the builder to see who knows the most about building. You hope he does. But you should be able to follow any conversation that involves your property. To that end I have included some basic information and diagrams illustrating the general structure and individual systems of houses, such as central heating. But it is only basic information and it goes without saying that it should not be used as a guide for any DIY activities. Use it to keep up with the builder, not to try to do his job.

Finally, I can't promise to convert you to the joys of property renovation, but I can show you how to work with your builder rather than against him, to achieve the results you want when you want them. Your property is probably your most valuable asset and it deserves your special attention. So read on – before you know it you'll be talking soffits and snots with the best of them.

CHAPTER ONE

Plan Your Work and Work Your Plan

'Men don't plan to fail, they fail to plan'
(*William J. Siegel*)

The key to successful renovation is thorough planning. So don't attempt anything without it! Your very first task is to determine exactly what you can achieve and that means reconciling your dreams with both practical and financial restrictions. This rule applies regardless of whether you are simply refitting the kitchen or renovating the whole house and without this groundwork you are almost certainly on course for disaster. While writing this book I have spoken to countless builders, surveyors and architects, and their most consistent complaint is about clients who don't give a clear brief or who keep changing their minds. And it stands to reason. If you don't know what you expect from the renovation, neither will your appointed agents – and that's when costs start to spiral out of control and disenchantment sets in. It is, therefore, essential that before doing anything else you spend some time clarifying your objectives. And for my money, this is actually the most rewarding part of home renovation, because it is where your personal input counts most. So, do you have pen and paper at the ready?

DEFINING YOUR OVERALL OBJECTIVES

Forget about money for a while (what a wonderful thought). Start by writing down absolutely everything that is relevant to your renovation, which is likely to incorporate:

The recommendations of the surveyor's report

If you have just purchased the property you will probably have had both a valuation and structural survey carried out. Most banks and building societies will insist on both, especially if the property has some age to it, although the information might be combined into one document (if you have lived in the property for some while and don't have a recent survey, now is the time to invest a few hundred pounds and have one done). The survey will include a lot of basic information on the number and size of rooms within the property, but there should also be a detailed list of the structural and cosmetic defects of the property and, if specifically requested, the surveyor's estimate of what these will cost to put right. Remember that the surveyor will only have noted 'visible' defects and there may be others which only become apparent when you start to take back the fabric of the property, e.g. those below ground level. But for the time being, list the suggested repairs, keeping them divided into repair/structural and the purely cosmetic. Depending on the age, style and condition of your property, the recommendations are likely to include some (or all) of the following:

Repair/structural
- Repair/rebuilding of any unstable walls, internal or external
- Repairing cracks, hairline fractures and loose areas in external rendering
- Repairing or replacing any other defective external features, e.g. split bricks, lintels etc.
- Replacement or modification of drainage systems
- Repair or replacement of roofing materials, including chimneys and guttering
- Attention to flat roof areas
- Insertion or replacement of damp-proof course
- Wet or dry rot treatment, for internal or external features (depending on whether or not the surveyor has picked up on it)

- Replacement of rotten floors, stairways and unstable ceilings
- Replacement of outdated or defective wiring
- Replacement of inadequate plumbing
- Installation or updating of heating system

Cosmetic
- Replacing features which are out of keeping with the style of the property, e.g. windows, doors and internal joinery
- External and internal redecoration, including plastering and painting
- Installation of new kitchen fittings
- Upgrading bathrooms and other sanitary installations
- Improving storage, e.g. fitted wardrobes, and layout of rooms

At this stage you don't need to make any choices, just the distinction between what is urgent (i.e. repair and structural work) and what can wait until later, if necessary (i.e. cosmetic items).

Your personal 'must haves'

This is the fun part. Here you can run riot and compile a 'wish list', i.e. absolutely everything that you would do if time and money were no object. This is an important part of your planning, because even though it is unlikely that you will be able to afford everything, you have at least got it all on paper and can then decide what should take priority. Start with the big picture and work inwards. That is to say, look first at the number, type, position and size of rooms you want, then the particular requirements of each. Ask yourself the following questions:

Number and type of rooms
- How many of the following do I want? (Bear in mind both the current and future requirements of your family.)
  - bedrooms
  - reception rooms
  - bathrooms
- Do I want to combine rooms? (E.g. kitchen and dining area, sitting and dining room, etc.)
- Do I want to change the use of any rooms? (E.g. a store room to a nursery, a loft to a bedroom/bathroom)
- Do I want to introduce any of the following extras? (E.g. a study/

library, utility room, play room, sauna, store room, nursery, games room, dressing room)
- Do I want/need to make additions, either sideways or upwards? (E.g. a porch, extra storey, conservatory, garage or complete extension)

Position of rooms
- Which rooms have to be close to one another? (E.g. bathrooms and bedrooms, kitchen and utility room, kitchen and dining room, etc.)
- Which rooms should be at the front and which at the back of the house? (E.g. the sitting room at the front, dining room at the back)
- Do some rooms need to be in a quiet area? (E.g. nursery, study, bedrooms)
- Which floor should rooms be on? (E.g. reception rooms on ground floor, bedrooms on first floor)
- Which rooms would benefit from morning or afternoon light? (E.g. afternoon light for a sitting room)
- Which rooms would benefit from having the best view?
- Do I need access to the garden and from which room?

Size of rooms
- Do I want to divide up existing rooms to create more units? (E.g. ensuite bathrooms, more bedrooms, etc.)
- Do I want to open up space by creating through rooms? (E.g. sitting room to dining room, or by removing cupboards from a landing)
- Do I want to use dead space? (E.g. by creating a loft conversion, adapting an understair cupboard)

Particular requirements of each room
- Do I want to update facilities? (E.g. have a better kitchen, refitted bathroom, install a laundry/utility room)
- Which rooms do I want to redecorate and does this include new joinery? (E.g. mouldings, architraves, dado rails, etc.)
- Do I want to create more light in certain rooms? (E.g. by increasing the size of windows, creating a light well, raising ceilings, increasing the capacity of the electrical system)
- Do I want to increase storage in any of the rooms?
- Do I want built-in cupboards and units in bedrooms, bathrooms or kitchens?

- Do I need special facilities (especially for the elderly and infirm)? (E.g. stair lift, bath supports, etc.)

General requirements
- What security features do I want? (E.g. door and window locks, alarm system, unbreakable glass, etc.)
- What heating system do I want? (see Chapter Five for more detail)
- Do I need more power points? (see Chapter Five for more detail)
- What safety features do I need? (E.g. child-proof windows, doors, electric sockets, etc.)
- How many telephones do I need?
- Do I want to alter the outside of the property? (E.g. the roof tiles, windows, doors, wall treatment and colour, etc.)

Although you are making general observations you should none the less record them in as much detail as possible, ideally room by room. You may not yet have decided on the exact style and position of fittings and you may not realise the full technical implications of what you are requesting, but at this stage it doesn't really matter. The important thing is to try to lay down clearly what you want done and start creating a list of works. For example:

Bathroom
- Existing bath, basin and loo to be removed and replaced with new fittings.
- Existing tiles to be removed and replaced with new tiles.
- Existing wood panelling to be stripped down and painted.
- Floor carpet to be removed and replaced with vinyl flooring.
- Spotlight to be removed and recessed ceiling light to be installed.

Sitting room
- Whole room to be redecorated – walls, ceiling, woodwork.
- The window to be converted to a door leading into the garden.

Dining room
- Create opening in wall for an archway through to sitting room.

Cupboard under the stairs
- To become downstairs cloakroom.

Study
- To become fourth bedroom with connecting door to adjacent bathroom.

Kitchen
- Existing kitchen to be removed and replaced with new units and appliances.
- Walls to be tiled.
- Floor to be tiled.
- Ceiling to be painted and new ceiling light fitted.
- Create serving hatch through to dining room.

External
- House to be repainted.

If you are really unsure as to how to describe a job, you can always approach it the other way round and describe the effect that the work should have, e.g. 'to allow the fireplace to be used again for log fires', and then let the builder advise you on the best way to achieve that result.

Lastly, don't be too worried at this stage about the cost implications of the above. This first part of the process is just a paper exercise and the paring down will follow.

GETTING A SECOND OPINION

It may seem a little cruel to shatter your dreams so soon, but once you have marshalled this information it is time to look at any possible restricting factors, which will in turn affect your list of works. For most people the greatest impediment is one of money, so start by taking both your structural survey and list of works to the professionals and ask for:

A location assessment

This applies if you are keeping strict tabs on resale value – and most people are! There is always the danger of over-investing in your house in relation to the neighbourhood; some properties fail to return monies spent on them because the location and neighbourhood are such that the property will never sell for more than a given figure. So you should seek the services of a chartered surveyor (or an estate agent – even cheaper) on this one (see Chapter Two); get his estimated valuation once works are completed and compare that to house values in your area. If you are going way over the mark, ask his advice as to what you should abandon. In other words, unless you really aren't worried about resale value, be prepared to forsake that billiard room!

Advice on maintenance

You might think this premature, but the ongoing cost of maintaining your renovation works should be taken into account right from the planning stage. It can go both ways – the cost of maintaining a swimming pool might make you think twice about having one, whereas installing proper roof insulation can actually save on future heating bills. Again, a surveyor can advise you.

A costing on the project

Depending upon the complexity of your renovation works, the costing might have to include the services of an architect (see Chapter Two) or surveyor and this has to be taken into account. However, the main expense is likely to be the building works and ideally you should go straight to a builder for these costings, as he will actually be doing the work. If you ask an architect or surveyor, they will only have to go and ask a builder themselves! We shall look at the business of choosing a builder and costing work in much greater detail in Chapter Three. Suffice to say here that once you have chosen your man and given him a list of works, there are four golden rules:

1. Examine the initial quote

The first and most important piece of information you need is a detailed breakdown of the cost of each element of your renovation works, which is why I advised you, in addition to the surveyor's report, to produce a room by room breakdown of jobs for the builder to quote against. Unfortunately, unless you are related to the Rothschilds, there will almost certainly be need for some modification to the initial quote: the figure given will be more than you expected. The harsh reality is that there has to be a system of priorities – hence rule 2 below.

2. Prioritise

You will need to seek guidance from your builder and/or surveyor but you should:

■ put structural and repair works before cosmetic and aesthetic improvements. The former are obviously more important and if you are just purchasing the property, might even be a requirement of your mortgage conditions; painting and decorating can be done at any time whereas something like dry rot has to receive immediate attention.

■ work from the outside of the house inwards. The most important jobs by far are those which make the house dry, structurally secure and warm; so start with the roof and exterior walls. When the property is weatherproof you can start thinking about internal works. Your order of priorities (most important first) should be:
  - External work, including foundations, walls, roof, windows and doors
  - Internal structural works, i.e. walls, ceilings and floors, necessary for the safety of the building (which includes treatment for infestations and rot)
  - Wiring
  - Plumbing
  - Plastering
  - Bathroom and kitchen facilities
  - Internal joinery and decorations

In a perfect world all the above areas would be handled together for reasons of cost and minimum disruption. But if you have to make economies, anything which is making the property unsafe should take absolute priority.

3. Group together related tasks

If it is possible and not in complete contradiction to the above, always try to avoid double handling, i.e. working on the same type of job twice. Not only does this involve extra cost but also extra disruption and dust. The most obvious jobs to complete in one go when practicable are:

Brickwork, stripping and plastering
This causes maximum mess and dust and should therefore be got out of the way in one shot. Doing all your demolition and brickwork together also saves the cost of having to bring back the skip.

Electrics

Have all your wiring done at one time (or at least one floor or ring main at a time). Going back later for an extra socket costs proportionately much more, mainly because it involves cutting channels through plaster, which in turn involves redecoration.

Plumbing

If you are refitting, e.g. the kitchen, try to have all other pipework, e.g. for the bathroom, fitted at the same time. Both plumbing and electrics should be completed before starting on plaster work, simply because they sit behind the plaster and you don't want to have to start hacking it off again. (I am, of course, referring to wall finishes – your pipes should not be plastered into masonry walls.) If you are short of money you could hold back on some of the final fittings. For example, have the plumbing done up to first fix (i.e. everything up to and including plastering) and leave the second fix (i.e. installing the actual fittings) until later; you can have isolating valves fitted on practically any pipe end, which will allow you to bring the rest of the house on line without actually having to fit the bath, basin, etc.

4. See what scope there is for reducing costs

One way is to abandon or adapt any job with a high premium. What you want and what is technically possible may be two quite different things. The position of load-bearing walls may restrict internal remodelling, as can the position of existing plumbing. In reality, almost anything can be moved or changed, but the cost of awkward improvements is always much higher than straightforward works (quite apart from the increased disruption factor) – so, for example, you may have to abandon the idea of moving the loo to another part of the bathroom. What's more, introducing a highly individual element can actually reduce the value of the property, or at least be offputting to prospective buyers, e.g. an ornate spiral staircase or upper floor cut away to give extra height. In addition, you could ask the builder for suggestions on alternative, less costly options on fittings, e.g. a cheaper range of kitchen units, formica rather than wood or tiled work surfaces, chrome rather than brass taps, etc.

YOUR BUDGET

Having got an idea of what the job could cost and where savings might be made, you have to look at your financial resources and whether or not you are willing and able to borrow. Once you have done this you can decide how far the list of works has to be modified. Your main financial options are as follows:

Your own money

Depending upon the extent of your renovations, you might only have to dip into your own savings. Cash is a powerful tool when negotiating discounts so use it when you can. But don't leave yourself exposed and make sure that you have sufficient reserves both for building extras and for other possible emergencies.

Credit card

This might be an alternative if the job is a small one and the contractor accepts credit cards, or if you decide to buy materials on behalf of the contractor. Either way, it only makes sense if you pay off the whole amount when the statement arrives, thereby gaining a few weeks' free credit.

A bank loan or overdraft

If the renovation works are fairly minor, your bank may agree to an overdraft, which they will expect you to pay back within a few weeks or months. For larger amounts of money they will probably advise you to take out a personal loan, to be repaid over a few months or years.

Increasing your mortgage with your existing lender

This method is a popular and easy way of borrowing money for home improvements (although there is no tax relief on the loan), mainly because the interest rates can be very reasonable and the repayments are made over a number of years. Sometimes it is referred to as a home improvement loan or 'additional advance' and is handled as a separate account. The loan is a safer one from the mortgage lender's point of view, because they take the title deeds to your property and can repossess if you default on payments. The loan is added to the current mortgage and the two combined will not normally be more than the value of the property. If you don't have an up-to-date valuation, and the original loan plus the new one total more than a certain percentage (usually 75 per cent or above) of the last valuation, you may have to pay a mortgage indemnity premium on the balance above the stated percentage. You may also be charged an arrangement fee.

Remortgaging with a new lender

At the time of writing this is also a good alternative, with some very attractive fixed rate deals available, but you have to take into account all the administrative costs, which can be significant.

A second mortgage

That is, one from a different lender, likely to be a finance house. Shop around and compare deals. Also make sure that your lender is a member of the Finance and Leasing Association, which operates a strict code of practice. There are sharks around, so beware.

Through your contractor

This can be done but many builders don't operate such schemes, and those who do will charge dearly for it, because the loan is not secured on the property and is thus more risky for them.

You may end up using either just one or a combination of these options. Don't be tempted to borrow more than you can comfortably live with. It's far better (although slightly more costly in the long run) to do the renovation work in stages, giving yourself a financial breather in between, than to feel pressurised into doing the whole job at once. There are several reasons for being cautious:

The cost of works going up

Yours would be a house in a million (particularly if it is an old one) if the work didn't end up costing more than expected because of hidden faults.

Mortgage rate increases (or MIRAS going down)

Think back to 1988 when so many of us were rushing to buy, interest rates were about 7 per cent and we all thought property was a sure thing. Less than three years later many homeowners were struggling to keep up with increased repayments. Always be conservative when it comes to borrowing.

Illness or involuntary redundancy

Neither of these can normally be anticipated (although they can be provided for with mortgage insurance plans), but you want to avoid having to stop the job in mid-progress because you cannot make repayments on a loan. There is nothing more debilitating than living with a half-finished kitchen or bathroom, quite apart from the worry of completing the payments.

GRANTS

Before spending or borrowing, look to see if there aren't other ways of raising the money. Surprisingly, in this cash-strapped age, there are still grants available for property renovation, but with strict limitations upon exactly who qualifies for them and when. The main grant sources are Local councils. For historic buildings and conservation areas they are English Heritage, Welsh Historic Monuments/Cadw, N. Ireland Housing Executive, or Historic Scotland, Heritage Policy Group 3.

Local councils

In theory, local councils offer five main types of grants for renovation works. They can either be discretionary or mandatory, but will in any case always be dependent upon the level of funding available (which can, of course be nothing!). They are designed to give help to those least able to pay for works to their properties and are therefore means tested, the result of which is that you most probably wouldn't get the whole repair paid for. None the less, they are worth investigating and are as follows:

1. Renovation grants

These are for the improvement or repair of houses and for the conversion of houses into flats and are open to owner-occupiers, landlords and tenants – but with certain restrictions. The grant is intended to:

- bring a property up to a 'standard of fitness for human habitation', e.g. be structurally stable, free from damp, have an internal water supply and sanitation, and have adequate provision for lighting, heating, ventilation and the provision of food, etc. It is mandatory to owner occupiers (under some circumstances, to landlords as well).

- repair or improve a property 'beyond the standard of fitness'. This grant is discretionary, can be in addition to the grant above and covers jobs such as replacing rotten windows, unsafe electrical wiring, ineffective damp-proof course and repairing defective roofs, walls, foundations, staircases or floors.

- improve home insulation. This is discretionary and intended to encourage greater energy efficiency. Items covered include draught proofing, loft and water tank insulation.

- improve heating. Again, a discretionary grant, which can cover items such as central heating.

- 'provide satisfactory internal arrangements', i.e. to alter inconvenient or potentially unsafe features such as a very deep staircase or low doorway. A discretionary grant.

- aid conversions. Another discretionary grant, available for e.g. converting under-used houses or buildings into self-contained flats for letting.

2. Common parts grants

These are intended to help improve or repair the common parts of buildings containing one or more self-contained flats. This can include areas such as the roof, staircase and hallway. Common parts grants are normally discretionary and available to both landlords and occupying tenants.

3. HMO grant

Available to cover a wide range of works for houses in multiple occupation (HMO's) where the occupants are not part of a single household. The main purpose of the grant is to make the building fit for human habitation and the criteria are as before. This is normally a discretionary grant.

4. Disabled facilities grant

This is designed to tailor a disabled person's home to meet their special needs and can be granted to an owner-occupier, tenant or landlord on behalf of a tenant, but only after the council have satisfied themselves that the works are necessary and practicable.

5. Minor works assistance

This is a discretionary grant designed for small-scale works and for those receiving an income-related benefit or over 60 years of age. It covers things such as thermal insulation and improvements for elderly people (Age Concern publish a useful leaflet which details the help available to people over 60 years of age – see the Names and Addresses section at the end of this book).

The first step is to contact the renovation grants section of your local council to see whether or not there are any grants available and if you qualify. Start by reading the 'House Renovation Grants' booklet issued by the Department of the Environment and the Welsh Office, and then ask for more detailed advice. In N. Ireland the equivalent booklet is the 'Guide to Home Improvement Grants', available from the Local Grants Offices of the N. Ireland Housing Executive. In Scotland it is called 'Improve Your Home with a Grant', and is available from the local authority.

The system varies within the U.K., but for England and Wales it is as follows. You will automatically be ineligible if:

– your property was built or converted less than ten years before the date of your application;
– your property is a second home;
– the works are not considered essential, e.g. internal decoration.

Should you be eligible the council will give you a form to complete which will allow them to carry out a means test. Basically, this test looks at your weekly income and any savings over £5000. This figure is compared to their assessment of your basic needs. If your financial resources are less than the total of this assessment, you get a full grant. If your resources are more, they will deduct the proportion you are deemed to be able to afford from the total cost of works and award a grant to cover the balance (if any). You will be unlikely to get a grant if you start work before the council have formally approved your grant application. Once in place, you have a year to complete the works and must provide proper invoices against which the council can reimburse you (alternatively, you can ask the council to pay the builder direct). Responsibility for the standard of work lies with you and the council can ask for repayment if the work is not carried out satisfactorily. Lastly, if you are an owner-occupier or a landlord and sell your property within three or five years respectively, you may have to repay all or part of the grant.

English Heritage

English Heritage have grants available for historic buildings and houses within conservation areas. This last category is also covered by a special scheme pertinent to London boroughs, known as London Grants. Your property does not have to be listed to qualify, but it helps.

Historic buildings

Money is tight, and as a result your property has to satisfy strict criteria before a grant is awarded; the good news is that this doesn't involve any means testing. For an historic buildings grant your application will be assessed against the historic importance of the property, the urgency and nature of the work and the need for financial help. Basically, English Heritage want to make sure that the net value of your property after repair exceeds the cost of maintenance, alteration, conversion, improvement or demolition. There are sometimes conditions attached to these grants, such as allowing public access to the building.

Conservation areas

Conservation area grants are available for 'the repair of historic buildings which contribute to the character of the conservation area'. Again, assistance is confined to structural and external works, such as re-roofing, repairs to windows and doors, etc. and in some areas grants are conditional on local materials being used. Maintenance, alterations and conversions are not covered.

Grants do not normally exceed 40 per cent for historic buildings and 25 per cent for conservation areas, but larger grants are given if deemed necessary. The application forms are very straightforward and are available from the grants section of English Heritage, based in London (see Names and Addresses). Be aware that if you do not satisfy the condition of the grant or sell the property within ten years, English Heritage can ask for their money back! Lastly, English Heritage also publish a very useful directory of all public sources of grants for historic buildings which is well worth consulting (see the Reading List at the back of this book).

YOUR LIFESTYLE

Unfortunately, building costs aren't the only expense involved in renovating a property. Last but not least you have to consider your involvement in the renovation process – something which can have quite an impact on the cost of the job. Ask yourself the following questions:

How much time can I devote to managing the renovation?

I am assuming that, with the exception of any necessary technical input from, for example, architects and surveyors, you want to manage the day-to-day building works yourself. How far you can achieve this really depends upon how much work needs to be done and whether or not you have a full time occupation. If the works are relatively uncomplicated, i.e. mainly cosmetic, you could probably manage renovations from your place of work (given that most of the renovation will be carried out during working hours) with the aid of a telephone and some pre- or after-work site meetings. This does, however, depend somewhat on the nature of your work (and your boss!).

If the job is going to last several months and involve the whole gamut of electrics, plumbing, brickwork and plastering, you should be prepared to take time off, be called out for emergencies and generally have your timetable – work, social and domestic – turned upside down. Unless you can be this flexible and have a competent, reponsible builder, you might just need some help in managing the renovation process, which will, of course, add to your costs. The same applies, but even more so, if you are renovating a property from a distance; I chose to do so with a house 150 miles away and a demanding job – and redefined the meaning of stress in the process! But if you can be around the house a lot of the time, it it perfectly possible to manage most renovation works yourself. It is labour intensive but very rewarding and cost effective.

Where will I live while work is in progress?

Never underestimate the inconvenience of sharing your property with the builders. If they are working on just one or two rooms, you can isolate the mess, maintain some semblance of normality and stay in the property while work is in progress. If, however, they are working on the whole house and need to install a completely new electrical circuit/ heating system, etc., practically every room will be disrupted, which is not very convenient and is even potentially dangerous if you have children about the place. The worst scenario is that you might be left without heating, light or water and have to cook and wash with temporary equipment; or failing that, be forced to use the shower at the local swimming pool for your daily ablutions! Generally speaking, unless you are one of the lucky few who have another house to live in while work goes on, the options are as follows, in ascending order of expense:

- living on site in an isolated section of the property, maintaining services wherever possible – the cheapest and most practical solution if possible.

- living in the garden/nearby in a caravan – again, a good alternative if available and one which can sometimes reduce the cost of the job since you are not in the builder's way and are thus allowing him to work that much more quickly.

- renting rooms locally. This can be costly and means that your finger is not always on the pulse. But if you really want to have the works done while you are not in the property and haven't yet completed on the purchase, you could try to do so before completing on the sale of your current home, thus leaving a period in which the works can be carried out and you still have somewhere to live. You take a big risk in doing so as the sale might yet fall through and you will have wasted time, effort and money. Also, it might involve a bridging loan.

Figure 1. The Decision-Making Process

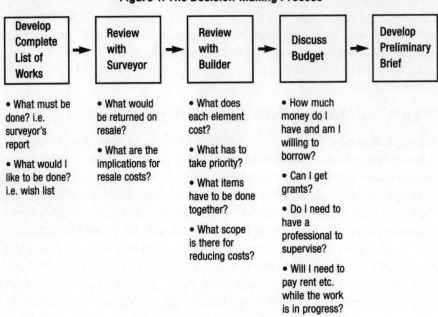

Develop Complete List of Works	Review with Surveyor	Review with Builder	Discuss Budget	Develop Preliminary Brief
• What must be done? i.e. surveyor's report • What would I like to be done? i.e. wish list	• What would be returned on resale? • What are the implications for resale costs?	• What does each element cost? • What has to take priority? • What items have to be done together? • What scope is there for reducing costs?	• How much money do I have and am I willing to borrow? • Can I get grants? • Do I need to have a professional to supervise? • Will I need to pay rent etc. while the work is in progress?	

■ going on an extended holiday (and leave the builder unsupervised, are you kidding?!) – only for the rich and trustworthy/foolish.

In other words, the consideration of where you live not only has significant bearing upon the costs of the renovation and thus on what you can afford to do, but also on how easy it will be for you to take part in managing it.

The whole of the above decision-making process can be illustrated by means of a flow chart (see Figure 1).

PRODUCING YOUR PRELIMINARY BRIEF

Figure 1 will help you draw up a budgeted list of works, laid out in order of priority (see Figure 2). The budget on page 24 has been drawn up in such a way that you can easily discriminate between what is essential and what can wait (see the Key).

I can almost guarantee that the final bill will be bigger than your total budget figure, simply because renovations have a habit of throwing up unforeseen problems! So you should really hold back 10 per cent for surprises, i.e. if you have £20,000 to spend, only allow £18,000 for total budget at this stage and expect to incur the other £2,000 as you go along. That done and armed with your list of works, finance and a healthy dose of resolve, you are now ready to commence battle.

Figure 2. Budget Work Sheet

(A) Task	(B) Cost	(C) Option	(D) Linkage with other tasks
1. Install damp proof course	£1500	N/A	Takes 1st priority
2. Rewire whole house	£5000	£4000	After 1. and 5.
3. Install new kitchen	£7000	£5000	Ideally at the same time as 2 but not essential
4. Fit new ensuite bathroom	£4000	£3000	
5. Treat damp and replaster nursery	£700	N/A	Before 2. and after 1.
6. Paint outside of house	£1000	£300	Any time after 1.
(H) Rent			
(I) Architect/ Surveyor			
(J) **TOTAL BUDGET**			

KEY TO CATEGORIES

A. List of the tasks

B. This is the cost quoted for the task as you initially described it.

C. This is the builder's advice as to the lowest cost option. In some cases, e.g. damp-proof course, there is no cheaper alternative. But in others, such as painting the outside of the house, you could decide just to have the woodwork painted and leave everything else for another year or so, thus providing an option should you need to find savings somewhere.

D. This specifies the order in which the works have to be done, i.e. what has to be completed before other jobs can be started. So if you need to eliminate something for reasons of cost, make sure it's not a job necessary for any subsequent jobs. You should also take into account here the grouping together of similar tasks, e.g. all electrical work, plastering etc.

E. These are top priority jobs – those which cannot wait (and for which often there isn't any

(E) Immediate	(F) As soon as possible	(G) Anytime	TOTAL
£1500			
£4000			
	£5000		
	£3000		
£700			
		£300	
£1500			
£2000			
(K) £9700	(L) £8000	(M) £300	**£18,000**

lower cost option), although I have shown an example of electrical wiring, where you could just opt for fewer sockets.

F. These are items which you doubtless want most of all, but which don't affect the safety of your home and thus could wait if necessary. They are also prime targets for cost cutting – you didn't really want that jacuzzi for eight, did you?

G. These are the least important jobs of all, normally cosmetic, and take the lowest priority.

H. Rent – if it applies, it has to be included in the overall budget.

!. Again, professional fees have to be added in.

J/K/L/M. You have now created sub-totals for what is immediate, what is fairly pressing, and what can be done at any time – the idea being that you only add in the latter two categories if after the 'immediate' column you still have budget to spare; you now know exactly what it is you want the builder to do. The end figure is your total budget for the job, and should not be more than your available finance.

CHAPTER TWO

The Professionals

'Too many cooks spoil the broth'

So, you have established what you want to achieve and how much you can spend. But as I have already mentioned, you also have to consider what professional assistance you will require. The shortest chain of command is that of client to builder, which we shall look at more closely in Chapter Three. But depending upon the scale and complexity of the work, you may first need to employ other professionals – surveyor, architect, structural engineer, project manager, architectural technician – and it is essential that you know when they are each necessary . . . and when they are not! The right choice of professional help can save you time, aggravation and money – quite apart from ensuring that your property renovation is structurally sound and aesthetically pleasing. But the choice can be confusing.

Jack of all trades

Perhaps the single most important point to remember is that there is absolutely no legislation that says you have to employ any of the aforementioned people for any aspect of property renovation and in the real world a good builder may well be all you need – it is simply a matter of requirement and personal choice. Ultimately, your decision on whom you employ will depend upon:

- the nature and complexity of the works;
- your budget;

- how comfortable you feel with that person – a factor not to be underestimated. You may well end up choosing one over the other simply because you get on together.

One of the great frustrations of deciding whether or not you need to use someone and if so, whom, is that these days everyone declares themselves able to handle just about everything – from initial drawings to paying off the builder. This is all part and parcel of the need to be competitive, but that doesn't help the poor confused property owner who just wants to make an informed choice. The truth is that most good professionals are capable of handling all the phases of a property renovation, but they will each specialise in a slightly different aspect and consequently have a different scale of charges. The likely scenario is that you won't want everything done for you, just the areas you don't feel competent to manage, and it seems a waste of a professional's talent and of your money to ask an architect to find a builder if you could do so yourself. So don't let anyone bully you into accepting their whole package – pick and choose the bits you want done for you. Remember too, that the customer is king and that fees are almost always negotiable. One thing you can be sure of, with the property industry having suffered such a hammering in recent years, they will all be pleased to see you!

THE SURVEYOR

Most of you will only ever have met a surveyor in the context of buying a property and having a structural survey done. And that is usually where the relationship ends. What you probably don't know is that a surveyor can play a significant role in property renovation, but just to complicate matters there is more than one type of surveyor and you have first to determine which one you might need and when.

Choosing the right one

The Royal Institution of Chartered Surveyors (RICS) recognises seven different fields of specialisation. The three most relevant to property renovation are:

- general practice surveyors, who tend to focus on property valuation work, i.e. at the pre-purchase stage
- quantity surveyors, who get involved during the renovation process but usually in large projects (say over £250K) and specifically to control the cost of works.
- building surveyors, the ones you are most likely to use for renovation works and who can, if necessary, guide you through the whole process.

You should always opt for a 'chartered' surveyor, as this guarantees their professional status and should also ensure competence. Membership of the RICS or the ISVA (Incorporated Society of Valuers and Auctioneers) is another good sign as these bodies lay down a code of conduct designed to protect the client's interests. They publish a directory of members (see back of book for address) which will indicate who is local to you. Feel free to ask for references and compare two or three surveyors before making a decision.

What a building surveyor can do

A building surveyor can advise on or administer the repair, alteration and renovation of buildings. So if your aim is principally to tidy up the property, make a few small changes, e.g. a through lounge, but to concentrate on remedial works rather than new designs, a chartered building surveyor could well be the most appropriate choice. While he won't have the specific structural and design knowledge of a structural engineer and architect respectively, he will have enough general experience to cope with most property renovations – a 'mud to rafters' man, if you like! I will stick my neck out and say that for the average property renovation (if there is such a thing), if you need any professional help at all (other than that of the builder) it is most likely to be from a chartered building surveyor.

The RICS 'Building Works' document defines the potential role of a chartered building surveyor in great detail. Broadly, however, it is as follows:

1. To meet with the client and discuss their renovation requirements. Quite often this is not on site.

2. To visit the property, carry out a full inspection and then give the client advice on exactly what works are needed, approximate costs,

which other professionals they might need to involve and how long it will all take. The surveyor then carries out a 'measured survey' of the property, i.e. measures it up so that accurate floor plans can be drawn.

3. To prepare 'sketch proposals', i.e. outline drawings for the alterations. This preparation becomes especially important if the client is unsure of what he wants, as it spells out the full extent of the works and thus the likely scale of cost.

4. If given the go-ahead by the client, to prepare 'final drawings'. There can be several different versions of these, depending upon the scale of the renovation; one set for planning approval and one set for building regulations (if needed, see Chapter Four); and possibly two more sets for the builder – one to show any structural alterations needed and another to demonstrate the layout of services, i.e. electrics and plumbing – trying to get everything on to one piece of paper can get very complicated! If the works are straightforward, you might well find that the building regulations drawings double up for the builder, since they are the essential instructions which allow the builder to satisfy Building Control.

5. To submit applications for planning and building regulation approval.

6. To write a final detailed specification of what needs to be done and the cost involved (or get a quantity surveyor to do so, depending upon the size of the job) and then to invite firms to tender for the work, i.e. quote for it.

7. To prepare contract documents for signature by the client and contractor.

8. To monitor the quality and progress of the work on site, manage the payments to the contractor and to see the project through to its conclusion, when a 'practical completion certificate' is issued.

What building surveyors charge

There is no official fee scale for building surveyors and it is up to the individual to quote. Generally speaking, they work on a percentage of the contract value (i.e. the cost of the building works), roughly 10 per cent, but the smaller the contract the higher the percentage! The RICS publish a set of professional charges, but these are only recommended, not mandatory. This is a very competitive market and you can negotiate. Avoid an hourly charge – it always seems to lead to resentment because the surveyor does have to make site visits, sometimes unexpectedly, and the client inevitably feels that this is an area open to exploitation.

More and more clients are requesting a fixed fee, especially if they only want the surveyor to handle one aspect of the contract. This is good for you but potentially hazardous for the surveyor. In return they will want you to be very specific in stating what you want (go back to Chapter One) so that they know exactly what their fee covers. The lump sump will be calculated by multiplying their hourly rate by the time they think the job will take. A surveyor working from home with no overheads can charge as little as £20 per hour. But expect to pay up to £100 per hour for a large firm. Remember to ask if the initial discussions are free of charge; they often are. And don't forget to check whether or not the agreed fee includes expenses.

The 'Sting'

You will probably use a surveyor to represent your interests at just some of the stages listed above and the RICS 'Building Works' document divides them into 'preliminary', 'precontract' and 'postcontract' sections for that very purpose. But bear in mind that most surveyors (and architects) will try to load their fees up front to allow for this possibility. As much as 75 per cent of the total fee will be quoted for the 'preliminary' and 'precontract' stages. This is quite disproportionate to the amount of effort that goes in – by far the most labour intensive part of the process comes later when monitoring the contractors, the stage you are least likely to use them for. But to make this look like good value for money and to encourage you to use them for the whole process, they often allocate only 25 per cent for postcontract services. You have been warned – use this knowledge to negotiate accordingly!

Contracts

Depending on how much of the renovation you have employed your surveyor to manage, he may produce either or both of the following forms of contract:

- The JCT Agreement for Minor Building Works, 1980 Edition (see Figure 3). This is an all-encompassing sixteen-page document, recommended for building jobs up to the value of £70K (at 1987 prices), which defines your agreement with the 'contractor', i.e. the builder, in great detail but only mentions the surveyor (or architect) in his role of administering the contract once on site. From the surveyor's point of view, it is important because it defines the builder's obligation in full (clause 1.1), and pretty much reduces the duty of the building surveyor (or architect) to noticing the fact that the builder has done something defectively, not preventing it in the first place.

- A contract specifically between surveyor and client. There are various examples, one available from the RICS which is a basic form of agreement supplemented by the Building Works 'Scopes of Service' sheet (which details the exact services you require of the surveyor). Alternatively, you might just be offered a simple letter of agreement, especially if you have asked the surveyor to handle just one aspect of the job, such as plans.

Whichever form of contract you have, make sure you read and understand all the clauses and small print before signing. If there is a clause you don't like, ask for it to be struck out or amended to something you can live with.

Disputes and insurance

The two areas most likely to cause dispute are:

- the surveyor 'over certifying monies', i.e. authorising payment in advance of works being properly completed and the builder then going bust.
- the surveyor giving design or building advice which later proves defective.

Surveyors have to carry insurance so you can claim against them. But first you should always try to sort out the problem person to person. If that fails, get another surveyor to give an independent opinion, especially if it is unclear as to who is at fault, the 'agent' or the builder.

Figure 3. JCT Agreement for Minor Building Works (extract)

Conditions hereinbefore referred to

1.0 Intentions of the parties

Contractor's obligation

1.1 The Contractor shall with due diligence and in a good and workmanlike manner carry out and complete the Works in accordance with the Contract Documents using materials and workmanship of the quality and standards therein specified provided that where and to the extent that approval of the quality of materials or of the standards of workmanship is a matter for the opinion of the Architect/the Contract Administrator such quality and standards shall be to the reasonable satisfaction of the Architect/the Contract Administrator.

Architect's/Contract Administrator's duties

1.2 The Architect/The Contract Administrator shall issue any further information necessary for the proper carrying out of the Works, issue all certificates and confirm all instructions in writing in accordance with these Conditions.

2.0 Commencement and completion

Commencement and completion

2.1 The Works may be commenced on

....

and shall be completed by

....

Extension of contract period

2.2 If it becomes apparent that the Works will not be completed by the date for completion inserted in clause 2.1 hereof (or any later date fixed in accordance with the provisions of this clause 2.2) for reasons beyond the control of the Contractor, including compliance with any instruction of the Architect/the Contract Administrator under this Contract whose issue is not due to a default of the Contractor, then the Contractor shall so notify the Architect/the Contract Administrator who shall make, in writing, such extension of time for completion as may be reasonable. Reasons within the control of the Contractor include any default of the Contractor or of others employed or engaged by or under him for or in connection with the Works and of any supplier of goods and materials for the Works.

Damages for non-completion

2.3 If the Works are not completed by the completion date inserted in clause 2.1 hereof or by any later completion date fixed under clause 2.2 hereof the Contractor shall pay or allow to the Employer liquidated damages the rate of £ .... per ....[b.4] between the aforesaid completion date and the date of practical completion. The Employer may deduct such liquidated damages from any monies due to the Contractor under this Contract or he may recover them from the Contractor as a debt.

Completion date

2.4 The Architect/The Contractor Administrator shall certify the date when in his opinion the Works have reached practical completion.

Defects liability

2.5 Any defects, excessive shrinkages or other faults to the Works which appear within three months [c]

....

of the date of practical completion and are due to materials or workmanship not in accordance with the Contract or frost occurring before practical completion shall be made good by the Contractor entirely at his own cost unless the Architect/the Contract Administrator shall otherwise instruct.

The Architect/The Contract Administrator shall certify the date when in his opinion the Contractor's obligations under this clause 2.5 have been discharged.

3.0 Control of the Works

Assignment

3.1 Neither the Employer nor the Contractor shall, without the written consent of the other, assign this Contract.

Sub-contracting

3.2 The Contractor shall not sub-contract the Works or any part thereof without the written consent of the Architect/the Contract Administrator whose consent shall not unreasonably be withheld.

Contractor's representative

3.3 The Contractor shall at all reasonable times keep upon the Works a competent person in charge and any instructions given to him by the Architect/the Contract Administrator shall be deemed to have been issued to the Contractor.

Exclusion from the Works

3.4 The Architect/The Contract Administrator may (but not unreasonably or vexatiously) issue instructions requiring the exclusion from the Works of any person employed thereon.

Architect's/Contract Administrator's instructions

3.5 The Architect/The Contract Administrator may issue written instructions which the Contractor shall forthwith carry out. If instructions are given orally they shall, in two days, be confirmed in writing by the Architect/the Contract Administrator.

If within 7 days after receipt of a written notice from the Architect/the Contract Administrator requiring compliance with an instruction the Contractor does not comply therewith then the Employer may employ and pay other persons to carry out the work and all costs incurred thereby may be deducted by

[b.4] Insert 'day', 'week' or other period'.

[c] If a different period is required delete 'three months' and insert the appropriate period.

THE ARCHITECT

What architects do

The architect's main function is to advise the client on the best and most elegant ways of altering or adding on to their building. Their particular skill is one of design and the manipulation of space. A good architect will:

- help the client define his priorities and limitations;
- interpret the client's requirements into designs;
- use his professional expertise to improve upon the client's ideas wherever possible.

In other words, if you are looking for detailed creative input you might well need to employ an architect – as opposed to a building surveyor, whose main function is to organise works.

In addition, an architect can handle the subsequent stages of property renovation, namely:

- discussions with the client
- carrying out a measured survey
- sketching proposals
- creating plans and drawings
- submitting planning and building regulations applications
- preparing a detailed specification
- putting the work out to tender
- preparing contracts
- monitoring the builder and other contractors and making payments

How to find a good one

Be aware that almost anyone can call themselves an architect, although they shouldn't unless properly qualified. To protect yourself you should always look for a 'chartered' architect, registered with the Architects Registration Council of the United Kingdom (ARCUK). A chartered architect has to study for at least seven years before qualifying and that should give you some idea of the depth of knowledge they are required to achieve before actually being let loose on a building. Ideally, they should also belong to a professional body such as the Royal Institute of British Architects (RIBA) or the Association of

Consultant Architects (ACA), both of which operate strict professional codes of conduct.

You should always compare two or three architects before making a choice. Refer to RIBA or the ACA for a recommendation, ask among your friends or even a local estate agent. Look for one who specialises in property renovation and whose general style (if discernible) appeals to you. Request references and don't be afraid to follow them up. Try also to use a local architect; not only will he be easier to contact and meet, but he might have knowledge about your borough development plan which could help in planning and building applications. Lastly, take time to chat with each 'candidate'; it is vital that you feel some positive chemistry, because you will be working together closely during the briefing and initial design stages.

What they cost

Most architects will want to charge a percentage (usually about 10 per cent) of the overall value of the contract or an hourly rate, both of which practices can be abused. You will also find that fees are higher for renovation than for new building. The RIBA publishes a recommended scale of fees, which I would use *only* as a platform for negotiation – don't accept them outright. In case you think I am being a little bit unfair, note that a few years ago The Office of Fair Trading investigated RIBA's 'monopoly' of fees. You really have to be firm with these chaps. I would try to agree a lump sum instead, especially if the architect was only handling part of the project, e.g. drawing up designs. The architect might well calculate this by multiplying the estimated number of hours for the job by his hourly rate; the latter can vary from £130 per hour for a partner in a city practice right down to £20/30 per hour for someone self-employed. In the current climate you can undoubtedly get a good deal. If negotiations aren't going well, be prepared to walk away or at least casually mention the number of unemployed architects looking for commissions. That should do the trick.

Make sure you understand the terms of payment. It is quite normal for the architect to invoice you in stages, e.g. monthly, rather than in a lump sum at the end of the contract.

How to brief your architect

This is where the problems often start. I have nothing against architects – some of my best friends are ... No, seriously, there is sometimes a tendency among architects to consider themselves at the top of the professional tree and superior to everyone else, including the client. They may consider this fair recompense for the seven years it took to earn their stripes. But there is a danger of being so overawed that you forget to mention what it is *you* want. Even when you do, some architects seem to have difficulty listening to their clients.

The secret of success is communication. On the one hand the architect is not a servant. You are paying a premium for his specialist skills and should expect his knowledge to be a big contributive factor in getting the work done. Learn to listen to that advice. On the other hand, you should always make your own wishes clear and intervene if you think that the architect is deviating from your brief for no good reason. Above all, discuss every detail until you are happy. Note that RIBA produces a free leaflet called *Working With Your Architect on Smaller Building Projects*.

Contracts

RIBA produces a Standard Form of Agreement for the Appointment of an Architect – SFA/92 – 'a set of documents which, taken together, should enable architect and client to express formally and unequivocally the agreement reached between them'. In other words, this is a standard Memorandum of Agreement in conjunction with 'Schedule Two' which details the services to be provided by the architect. In addition, he will probably produce the JCT Agreement for Minor Building Works. The ACA produces an alternative to the JCT Minor Works contract, called the ACA Form of Building Agreement 1982, which purports to be simpler and more client-orientated (easier to understand!) Its main strength is that it very clearly defines the responsibilities of the architect, builder and client and has a number of key optional clauses which allow the document to be very closely tailored to each individual building project. Depending on the scale of the job you could be asked to sign more than one of these agreements.

Before signing anything make sure you have read all the small print.

The SFA/92 contract is sometimes criticised for coming down in favour of the architect and protecting him from any failure on the part of the builder. Having said that, a lot of care has gone into preparing the documents and they are likely to be better than a home-concocted version. The answer is probably to use them but agree to strike out or amend any clauses you are not happy with.

Note that there are now two alternative forms of the JCT contract for use where a renovation grant is made available by a local authority for eligible work – one where the client owner or occupier engages an architect to administer the grant-aided work (Form RG(A)), and the other where the client deals directly with the builder (Form RG(C)). These are available from, among other places, the RIBA publications department.

Disputes and insurance

You are fully entitled to expect your architect to conduct himself professionally and in your best interests. If he is negligent, e.g. by designing something later proven to be either unsafe or impractical, you might well be able to sue him – although it is unlikely that any major technical faults would have got past building regulations. Note that not all architects carry professional indemnity insurance, mainly because of its prohibitive cost. But obviously from your point of view it is preferable to choose one who does in the event that you need to make a claim. Some contracts, such as the ACA version, include provision for appointing an independent adjudicator should there be a dispute.

THE STRUCTURAL ENGINEER

What they do

The role of structural engineers is basically to make things stand up. Their training teaches them about the infrastructure of buildings and how to calculate the necessary size/strength of the various supporting structures that are needed to make a building stable and secure. This can range from the foundations of a house to the lintel over a door. Interestingly, the profession of structural engineer is one of the oldest in the building industry; Christopher Wren was one of the more famous – architects didn't exist as such in his day!

When you might need one

If your renovation is complex and structural, involving new openings, bigger windows, or extensive internal remodelling, you might well need an engineer to handle the mathematical calculations involved. This might encompass new building, e.g. an extension, or simply renovation works due to rot, cracks or unstable foundations. It is, however, fair to say that most people do not go directly to a structural engineer. They are more likely to start with a surveyor or architect, who will then subcontract to an engineer if necessary. But for those of you who have some knowledge of building and design and want help specifically with the structural calculations and inspection of structural work, it is another option. Should you want them to handle other aspects of the renovation, such as technical drawings, many will do that too.

How to find a good one

Your first approach should be to the Association of Consulting Engineers, regarded by many as the most prestigious association within this field. They publish an annual directory of member firms which lists companies by name and geographical location. Supplement this by personal recommendations and/or look in your local business directories. If at all possible find someone local, because any travelling they do on your behalf will be charged for (this goes for anyone you employ). Always cross check that they are members of the Association. Also ask whether or not they have personal indemnity insurance; a structural engineer is under no obligation to have it, and at several thousand pounds a year many of the smaller operators (often the ones who take on domestic renovation work) choose not to. But, once again, from your point of view having insurance obviously makes sense.

What they charge

The ACE publishes a recommended scale of fees, depending on the complexity of the work. This can either be a percentage of the value of the whole job, an hourly charge or a lump sum. For a small job (say

£50,000 or under), you could expect to pay up to 15 per cent. Hourly charges vary, depending on the size of the firm and seniority of the engineer, and can be anything from £20 to £150. You might feel more comfortable with a lump sum agreement, but quite often with structural alteration works, where so many factors are unknown, the engineer won't be so keen. Try anyway. If you do agree a set fee, make sure that you know exactly what it represents; on small jobs and especially where the budget is tight, the engineer simply can't afford to visit the site every day. So if that sort of control is important to you, be prepared to pay for it.

Depending on the size of the job and its duration, you will either be asked to pay up in full on or slightly before completion, or by instalments as works progress.

Contracts

Again, the ACE publish a recommended format of agreement, but for most small domestic jobs you are much more likely to be sent a simple letter stating the terms of the job. What's more, most structural engineers (and for that matter, architects and surveyors) wouldn't be interested in an agreement worded by you, if only because they would have to pass it to their solicitor to make sure it conforms for insurance purposes. Sometimes you just have to go with the flow!

Disputes

The ACE can recommend an independent arbitrator, or alternatively, the Chartered Institute of Arbitrators can nominate someone. If you do have a claim, this is when you'll be glad you chose an engineer with insurance.

THE PROJECT MANAGER

Project managers are a relatively new phenomenon in the building industry. While surveyors, architects, engineers, etc., will happily manage the builder on your behalf, somebody had the bright idea of creating yet another stage in the renovation chain by managing the person who manages the builder. In other words, project management is the 'overall planning, control and coordination of a project, from inception through to completion, on behalf of a client' (Architects and Surveyors Institute definition).

There are some reasonable arguments for using a project manager:

- They are not involved in any aspect of the actual building process and can therefore concentrate solely on making sure that the job is completed on time, within budget and to an agreed standard.
- They are independent and claim not to indulge in kickbacks from builders and so on.
- They normally charge a flat fee during the construction period (rather than an hourly rate), so there is no financial conflict of interest.
- They can get trade discounts on appliances of up to 50 per cent, which are passed directly on to the client.

I have no particular problem with any of this and a project manager is a good idea for people with no time and a generous budget. But I cannot really see that a project manager offers anything really critical for those of you who want to handle the builder yourself. I would make it a condition of any contract, with a builder, surveyor or architect, that the work was completed on time and within budget. In practice it would be very difficult to know for sure whether or not a project manager had some deal going with a builder or architect – so this just boils down to trust. Charging a flat fee is fair enough, but it is yet another cost and I would want to see evidence of how this was offset by the savings being achieved for me. These savings might come via the discounts on supplies (which, incidentally, you can negotiate yourself), but I would be most surprised if you couldn't do the same deal with the architect or builder direct. In other words, I feel that project managers are best left to those who can afford the luxury of putting another layer of padding between themselves and the builder.

The only point I would concede is that a project manager might help in the initial stages when costings are being drawn up. It is important that the property owner knows what his financial liability is likely to be. It is also true that some architects don't have a firm grasp of the relation between plans and their effect on the cost of the project. So in that sense, if you were managing your own renovation you might want to ask a project manager to help draw up a list of all possible costings, so that you are fully aware of the potential liabilities. For this service you would normally pay an hourly charge. If you want to find out more, there is an Association of Project Managers (address at the back of the book).

Contracts

Apart from the ubiquitous JCT Minor Works form, you will probably be offered just a simple letter of agreement between you and the project manager.

Insurance and disputes

Project managers don't have to have insurance. Many consider it unnecessary because they really cannot be held liable for very much; the contract is between client and architect or builder, not between the client and project manager, who would have to instruct the builder to do something unsafe or illegal before he came into the firing line.

THE ARCHITECTURAL TECHNICIAN

Some people rather unkindly describe architectural technicians as the poor man's architect, those who didn't quite make it. They will not have taken the RIBA examination and are not chartered architects, although they will have an HNC or HND in Building Studies. But you shouldn't underestimate their ability. They can play a valuable role in property renovation and their skills are recognised by a number of banks and building societies. The industry body is called the British Institute of Architectural Technicians, who require full members to have at least five years of study behind them and two years of practical experience. It is a sensible precaution to check that anyone you consider using is a member and preferably a full one.

What they do

Architectural technicians 'specialise in the technological aspects of building design' (BIAT brochure). What this means is that they can produce a technically correct interpretation of an architect's design drawing (often for building regulations applications), but don't have the detailed construction knowledge of a structural engineer. They are really the modern equivalent of the old-fashioned draughtsman.

So, if your needs are more design-orientated, you probably want to choose an architect. If, however, you simply need someone to prepare drawings (either for planning/building regulations or just for the builder to work from) and offer advice, an architectural technician could be the answer. It's a useful halfway house between trying to do absolutely everything yourself and paying an architect's rates when some of his skills might be under-utilised. What's more, architectural technicians may be less qualified than architects, but some have extensive practical experience and can do pretty much everything that an architect can.

Surprise, surprise, the BIAT brochure tells us that architectural technicians can also handle all other aspects of property renovation, namely:

- Measured surveys
- Meeting with the client to discuss their requirements
- Producing sketch proposals
- Producing final drawings, both for planning and building regulations approval and for the builder to work from
- Making the planning and building regulations applications
- Inviting builders and other professionals to tender
- Administering the contract through to completion
- Producing post-building stage drawings and a maintenance manual, if required.

I suppose I shouldn't be so cynical, because they are just trying to be competitive, which is usually a good thing for the client, who benefits from better service and keener rates.

What they charge

The BIAT publish a recommended fee scale which suggests that for purpose-built residential accommodation charges should be based upon a percentage of the contract value – about 14.5 per cent for works worth £20,000 down to 11.5 per cent for a job worth £250,000. As always, this is open to negotiation. You might, for instance, prefer to agree to a lump sum, which could be worked out using an hourly rate. This is where you will notice a big difference in prices – architectural technicians charge from £15 per hour compared with an average of £50 per hour for many architects, but shop around, as prices vary greatly. What's more, competition is fierce, and you probably hold the trump card in any negotiation – that of simply going elsewhere. But also remember that these people are in business to make a living and a deal is only a good one if both sides are happy. So don't try to nail them (or any other professional) down too far – you simply won't get the service.

Contracts

You should have some sort of agreement in writing. If you are having something small done, like an extension, you might just be offered a letter of agreement. For larger works, the good old JCT Minor Works Contract is often used. In addition, the BIAT publishes a series of forms to be used in conjunction with JCT 80 throughout the contract period, one of which is the 'Confirmation of Instructions' (see Figure 4). This last-named is quite a useful document, especially as instructions do have a habit of changing throughout a job and these changes should be accurately recorded.

As with building surveyors' and architects' agreements, you will get confirmation of the cost and time of works, the exact nature of what has been agreed and so on; but an architectural technician will not assume responsibility for contractors who fail in their duty. I think the logic of it all is that you reduce the risk of employing a dud builder by going through an architect, building surveyor, or architectural technician, and this safety net forms part of their fee. On the other hand, if it all goes wrong they don't appear to carry any responsibility. In reality this doesn't happen very often, but the whole system could leave you feeling a little exposed.

Disputes and insurance

Should you have a disagreement, the Chartered Institute of Arbitrators has a procedure for the settlement of disputes between technician and client. Before appointing your technician check whether or not he has personal indemnity insurance – at a premium of £600 plus per annum, many don't.

Choosing the right person for the job is an essential part of your preparation – and no more so than with the builder, as we shall see in the next chapter.

Figure 4. Conformation of Instructions

BIAT

BRITISH INSTITUTE OF ARCHITECTURAL TECHNICIANS

Confirmation
of Instructions

Job No:

Practice Name:

Address:

Date:

To:

For:

I/We thank you for your instructions and confirm that I/we shall be pleased to act for you in connection with

I/We understand that I/we shall be responsible, under the terms of this agreement, for the following items which shall be carried out where applicable in accordance with the BIAT conditions of engagement dated 1st September 1987, as copy enclosed. I/We should be pleased to receive written confirmation from you that these conditions are acceptable.

Work Stages

Stage O: Survey
Stage A: Inception
Initial meeting with client to discuss brief and determine cost limits, to advise on the need for independent consultants such as Engineers, Quantity Surveyors, etc; and to give advice on possible types of contract and tender.

Stage B: Feasibility Studies
Preparation of sketch drawings to illustrate tentative proposals for discussion and development with client, and for preliminary discussions with authorities, etc.

Stage C: Final Scheme Drawings
Preparation of final scheme drawings and details; submission to client and suitable for submission under the Town and Country Planning Acts.

Stage D: Detail design
Commencing production information drawings for contractors use. Develop scheme to a stage suitable for submission under Building Acts, Regulations and other statutory requirements, and completion of applications for statutory approvals where necessary.

Stage E: Production information
Proceeding with production information including drawings, schedules and specifications suitable for the purposes of a tender.

Stage F: Contract preparation and administration
Inviting building contractors and specialist sub-contractors and suppliers to submit formal tenders and quotations for work. Considering offers received and making recommendations thereon to the client. Preparing contract documents as necessary and arranging for their execution. Giving instructions to appointed contractors on behalf of the client, inspecting work in progress to determine whether the contractor is fulfilling his obligations under the contract, carrying out other administrative duties entailed. Certifying interim applications for payment on account of work properly carried out, considering and agreeing final certificate of payment due under contract. Supplying client with set of "as built" drawings, service drawings and maintenance manual, if required. (For projects having a construction value of less than £20,000 this stage will be charged on a quantum meruit basis.)

Variations if applicable

The fees for carrying out this work will be £   at an hourly rate of £

at   % of the total contract sum (or estimated sum for abortive work) at an agreed lump sum of £

These fees are exclusive of prints, travelling, local authority fees and VAT. Accounts will be rendered in stages as work proceeds.

Signature

Principal/Partner/Director

SUMMARY OF PROFESSIONAL SERVICES

	Building surveyor	Architect	Structural engineer	Project manager	Architectural technicians
Structural survey	•	X	X	X	X
Preliminary advice	X	X	X	X	X
Costing a project	X	X	X	•	X
Measured survey	X	X	X	X	X
Sketch proposals	X	•	X	X	X
Architectural designs	X	•	X	X	X
Structural calculations	X	X	•	X	X
Planning/ Building reg. drawings/work ing drawings	X	X	X	X	•
Planning/ building reg. applications	X	X	X	X	X
Drawing up specifications	X	X	X	X	X
Tendering	X	X	X	X	X
Drawing up contracts	X	X	X	X	X
Monitoring works	X	X	X	•	X

KEY
X = can handle on behalf of the client (which might involve subcontracting to another party)
• = an area in which they specialise

CHAPTER THREE

The Builder

'A verbal contract isn't worth the paper it's written on'
(Sam Goldwyn)

Finding the right builder is central to the success of any renovation project and no more so than when you intend to deal with him direct. In a perfect world you would find someone who did the job on time, within budget, to a high standard, who understood the overall effect you were trying to achieve and lastly, was easy to communicate with. But alas, in this imperfect world the relationship between builder and client is often an uneasy one and, at the risk of making myself unpopular with you, I have to say that it is not always the builder's fault. Although bad builders definitely exist, you have an equally important part to play in the success of your renovation project, because it involves a working relationship between two people. Much depends on your making a good choice of builder in the first place and agreeing exactly upon what is to be done. But subsequent to that you have to achieve a fair and practical working arrangement which suits both parties. In other words, this renovation business works both ways.

FINDING THE RIGHT BUILDER FOR THE JOB

So, how should you go about finding that elusive creature, the reliable builder? There are several options:

Personal recommendation

This is one of the safest ways to find the right builder for your purposes. Someone else has effectively taken the risk first and found this person to be satisfactory. You can see for yourself the standard of work achieved (at least, on the surface) and get an honest opinion of what the builder was like to work with – was he on schedule, within budget, easy to talk to, and so on? The chances are that he will also be a local himself if he has been recommended by someone near by, and there are practical advantages to having a builder close at hand, especially if things go wrong or you need an emergency meeting.

Check, however, that your expectations are realistic. If your friend has lavished a lot of money on an extravagent renovation, you may be disappointed when the same builder cannot work miracles with your humbler budget. So do ask for personal recommendations, but also use your common sense to decide whether or not the jobs are comparable. You may need a builder who can draw up plans, whereas your friend just needed his house decorated. Look too at the type of renovation work that builder has carried out; he may, for example, be an expert in the problems of country cottages, but not so experienced or sympathetic with town houses.

Looking at other works being done in the locality

In essence this is another form of personal recommendation, except this time you look out for local properties that are being renovated and approach the owners to ask their opinion of the builder they are employing. Many people shy away from this option, mainly through inhibition. But I have never been turned away when asking for advice. Indeed, most people are only too happy to show you their home and share their experiences, good or bad. And since they don't know you it is a fairly safe bet that you will get an unbiased opinion. So be prepared to trawl your area and snoop around a bit in pursuit of recommendations – but check for angry dogs before you go waltzing into private property! And here is a hot tip. Always take a look at the builder's site. Is it tidy or is everything just lying about? A good builder will take care of his raw materials and keep them protected from the elements/opportunists when not in use.

Professional associations

There are several associations which exist to maintain good standards within the building industry. They each have a directory of members and will gladly send out a copy on request. The better known are: The Building Employers Confederation; The Federation of Master Builders, The Chartered Institute of Building and The Guild of Master Craftsmen. The advantage of using a member is that you know they have been vetted for overall professionalism, standard of work and in some cases, financial stability as well. It is therefore fair to assume that only a half decent builder would submit himself to such rigours in the first place. And if there are any problems the association can bring considerable moral pressure to bear upon the member, or even cancel their membership. A word of warning, though: don't assume that notepaper bearing a trade association logo is proof positive of membership of that association. Always double check that the person concerned really is a member.

As a further safeguard, some associations (including some representing specific trades, such as electricians and plumbers) operate guarantee schemes. The FMB, for example, have a very competitive warranty: for an extra 1 per cent on top of the gross contract price you are protected in the event of your member builder going bust during the contract or failing to complete the job properly. They will not only finish the job on behalf of the contractor but pay up to £10,000 of added costs (if applicable). They also give a five-year guarantee on work; the first two years for defective workmanship/materials and structural defects and the latter three years for structural defects only. The scheme also offers free conciliation in case of dispute and the institution of arbitration proceedings if necessary. This is a worthwhile investment.

There are also various independent insurance-backed guarantee schemes (involving the same 1 per cent deal or a one-off fee), so check whether your builder subscribes to any of the following:

■ *The Building Guarantee Scheme Ltd*
This operates in Scotland and Northern Ireland, covers disputes over the standard of workmanship on jobs valued between £500 and £100,000 and stays in force for a period of up to two and a half years after completion of the contract.

■ *The Independent Warranty Association*
This steps in if work is unfinished, substandard or the trader goes out of business. It covers the installation of windows, kitchens, bathrooms and conservatories.

■ *The Guarantee Protection Trust Ltd*
This pays for remedial work in the event of work being substandard or the builder ceasing to trade and covers treatment for woodworm, wet and dry rot and damp. It is in effect a guarantee on the builder's guarantee.

The best of all worlds

Possibly the very best way to choose a builder is to look for personal recommendation and then to double check if that builder is a member of a trade association. The recommendation could be from a friend, someone whose property you have admired or even from your local council. It probably isn't such a good idea to just turn to the Yellow Pages – anyone can advertise if they can afford it!

Whomever you consider, it is quite reasonable to ask to see their company accounts. After all, you want to know that they are stable and likely to be able to finish the job. (Incidentally, you are not alone. Some mortgage companies will ask for the name of the intended builder and then run a credit search on him.) No reputable company would refuse you that request and if they did, there might just be something to hide. You should also ask to see some of their work.

Learn to trust your instincts as well. Do you think you could communicate easily with this person? Do they seem honest, straightforward and knowledgeable? Would you be comfortable with the thought of them working in your house when you weren't there? Lastly, keep your options open. At this stage you should have two or three likely builders lined up, for reasons which will soon become clear.

COWBOY BUILDERS

'Cowboy (slang). A derogatory term for an often inadequately qualified person providing inferior services', *Chambers Twentieth Century Dictionary.*

Help from a cowboy is the one offer you definitely want to avoid. The only problem with cowboy builders is that you often don't know they are one until you have become a victim. Unfortunately they don't go round wearing a stetson advertising their status. But you none the less have to distinguish them from the many small operators (sometimes one-man bands) who are completely reputable. On first sight they might seem like any other builder and appear quite capable of handling all the various building processes you require. They will also play on the fact that most people are trusting and some are gullible. But there are some tell-tale signs you can look out for *before* commissioning any work and which should start your alarm bells ringing. A typical cowboy builder will *not*:

- always be registered for charging and paying VAT;
- normally offer properly written quotations;
- have an office address or official headed notepaper;
- be able to offer good references;
- carry Third Party insurance to protect the householder or the public;
- want to sign any sort of contract (however, he will want to be paid in cash, mainly to avoid paying taxes).

All of which you can discover before committing yourself in any way.

This is all well and good, but all sorts of good intentions fall by the wayside when faced with a 'bargain' and the cowboy builder's big carrot is often one of price. Despite all the warning signals you may still be tempted to consider using someone who appears much cheaper than all the rest, especially if you are on a very tight budget. Beware. You invariably do get what you pay for and as John Ruskin said, 'If you deal with the lowest bidder, it is as well to add something for the risk you run, and if you do that you will have enough to pay for something better.' Wise words. If you do give way to temptation, don't be surprised if your cowboy builder does *not*:

- employ properly trained labour;
- provide the standard of workmanship expected;

- provide redress in the event of complaints;
- comply with Health and Safety regulations.

You may also find that he slows down, turns up late or not at all and most important, finds reasons to charge much more than was originally agreed. But with no effective written agreement, you're stuck (and even if you have squeezed one out of him, it won't mean much if he suddenly goes bust and disappears, as frequently happens). In short, you are likely to end up with a more costly, yet lower quality job and in the worst instances, have to employ someone else to make good. If you're still not persuaded, ask at any Citizens Advice Bureau and they will oblige with some truly pitiful stories. And don't think that it's only the old and infirm who get caught – Chris Serle of the 'That's Life' television programme was one of their more famous victims! So don't necessarily go for the cheapest quote and always check out your builder's credentials. Otherwise it might cost a lot more in the long run – in money, time and stress. Stick to builders with a proven track record of good work.

GOING THROUGH THE BRIEF

Once you have identified two or three possible builders, make an appointment with each one individually to meet on site, i.e. at your house. Have your 'wish list' and surveyor's report to hand (although don't let the builder see any estimated costings in the latter), any plans or drawings that you may have had drawn up, and walk round the house together, going through the items in each. If necessary, do a dry run on your own before the builder arrives. Even if you are confident that you know what you want, ask for and listen to their professional advice. Few builders double as architects and interior designers, but a good one will have lots of technical and common sense advice about design and layout that you probably haven't thought of. So make use of it – you always have the option of rejecting it later on if the translation into money terms is unacceptable.

As you walk round make notes of what the builder is saying and amend your own list of works where appropriate (you may already have discarded one or two ideas as a result of discussions with a surveyor, see Chapter One). When you have met each builder and absorbed their advice, type or write up a final detailed description of the works – room by room is best, with a general section for works which affect the whole property, such as central heating and outside painting. This document is essentially a combination of what the surveyor has recommended, what you want and what the builder has advised, and it should be as comprehensive as possible, to help the builder give a fair and accurate price. Give a copy to each one (plus a copy of any relevant drawings) and ask them to come back with a costing. If they haven't already done so at the first meeting, they may want to come back and measure up to help them gauge an accurate price for items such as painting and carpentry.

So far this may seem pretty much one-sided, with you the client in the driving seat. But I think the situation is a lot more subtle than that. Your relationship with the builder is a crucial one and it has to get off to the right start. Your responsibility during this period is to show that you are a straightforward person who wants the job done properly and will pay promptly for it. Be quite up front about who else has been asked to tender, let each builder know that he is quoting on exactly the same list of works as the next man and agree clearly the date by which he has to submit his quote. If you do these three things, the builder is much more likely to feel he has a real chance of getting the contract and thus give a sensible price because:

- He knows whom he is competing against and that it is a reasonable number of people who are also of comparable skill and quality. (He might just name a silly figure if he thinks he is competing against a cowboy builder.)
- He knows that you have given the same specification and time limit to each party and are handling the contract in an organised manner. (Remember that builders don't charge for tendering and so cannot really afford to go chasing after jobs that are unlikely to be awarded to them.)
- He doesn't have to put up the price to include financing because you have already come across as someone who will honour a job well done and pay on time.

QUOTATIONS VERSUS ESTIMATES

Having told the prospective builders what you are doing, the next step is to compare the prices they submit. To do this you have to understand the difference between an estimate and a quotation and make sure that when looking at tenders you are comparing like with like; in everyday practice the two terms tend to get interchanged but actually mean quite different things and could materially affect your budget (but just so that you know, neither term has any definition in law).

A quotation

This is a firm price and what you can expect to pay for the specified works. It would be unusual for a builder to give a firm quotation on all parts of the renovation work, mainly because the nature of renovation means that you often uncover faults as you go along. You may well come across the phrase 'no provision has been made for unforeseen works', because no builder will want to commit himself to a price before he knows the full extent of the job. And if you insist on one, he will simply add 25–30 per cent to the job to cover all eventualities. So don't think you can win! But if the renovation work is more cosmetic than structural, or a combination of both, he may well be prepared to quote for the clearly definable aspects such as decoration, plastering, joinery, kitchen or bathroom installation, etc. These are all 'known quantities' and not likely to alter much as the result of other parts of the renovation.

An estimate

This is much less specific. Taking up a floor or investigating walls and ceilings might well bring to light damp or woodworm, and these could drastically alter the price of the job overall. So for anything involving excavation or structural work, the builder will only want to give an estimate, which is his best guess of what it will cost to carry out the client's wishes, subject to change as and when the nature of the job does!

A bit of both

Most renovation agreements will be part quotation and part estimate and this is acceptable so long as you insist on a detailed written breakdown of all aspects of the job. Never accept a document which gives a lump sum figure 'to renovate one house' (as if you would . . .). Insisting on a firm price can go against you, but it can equally have the virtue of flushing out the bad builders, because good ones will examine the site very carefully and discuss all possibilities before committing themselves to a final figure. If you like the builder but he is unhappy about the risk involved in quoting a fixed price, you could always agree to tackle problem areas as they occur, i.e. stop work, look at the problem and agree on the variation in time and price (in writing) before going ahead. But in general, get an 'exact and firm' quotation whenever possible – estimates only ever seem to go up!

THE SPECIFICATION

Each builder should then come back with a document detailing the work to be done and what it will cost. This is called the specification (often spec and pronounced 'spess'). The golden rule when managing your property renovation is to keep meticulous records of everything that is discussed. And the first and most important part of this documentation is the specification. You cannot possibly hope to remember all the detail and it is vital that both you and your builder have written documentation that can be used for reference, guidance and in the event of a dispute, evidence of what was agreed upon.

This document needs to be as comprehensive as possible and you should insist that it provides a breakdown of the various constituents of the job (ideally following the layout of your list of works), the price/ provision for each phase and, where relevant, the materials to be used (see Figure 5). The builder should go into much more detail than you did with your initial brief. For example, for point 1.7 you might well have said: 'To remove french windows and replace with Georgian-style doors', but look at the depth in which he describes it. You really have to insist upon and concentrate on the detail of a spec because:

Figure 5.

BUDGET PRICES FOR ALTERATIONS & REFURBISHMENT

1	**Roof Garden and Balcony**			
1.1	Investigate leak to front balcony around rain water outlet and increase the height of the flashing			373.00
1.2	Replace cover to roof tanks and redecorate			109.00
1.3	Replace all small section timber trellis including 4no. posts bolted to top of party wall			518.00
1.4	Redecorate the existing metal staircase and painted brickwork to the balcony and roof garden			428.00
1.5	Provide and fit 1no. external light adjacent to the existing outlet at the rear of the roof garden			103.00
1.6	Provide new TV aerial installation including cable to 4 no. internal points			675.00
1.7	Replace large sliding doors to balcony with two pairs of doors with fixed lights either side divided into smaller panes including double glazing, lead flashings and making good all surfaces disturbed			3970.00
1.8	Replace the 2 no. metal windows to the sitting room and kitchen with timber windows including double glazing, access scaffold and making good all surfaces disturbed			1779.00
	page 1 carried to summary			**£7,925.00**
	page 1			

- When looking at different specs you want to be able to make a fair comparison. One builder may be more expensive than another but only because he is being much more thorough.

- The builder's idea of what you asked for and your ideas of the same may be two very different things – so the key here is to get him to spell out every little detail. And don't be persuaded that this isn't necessary because the works are relatively minor: it is always necessary.

- The minute you give any builder the opportunity to take decisions on materials, size, finish, etc., disagreements are bound to follow and these items should always be fully described.

I can almost guarantee that when the spec arrives you will need a brandy. I always believe that the first spec is a tongue-in-cheek exercise on the part of the builder (even if it isn't, it helps me sharpen my pencil) and that he expects you to shave bits off. It doesn't matter how many times I go through the process, I am always horrified that my simple little requests can translate into such huge sums of money. That is until I start to go through the spec line by line and see just how much work I actually asked the builder to quote on. Now you have to sit down and go through the prioritising exercise with the builder – what has to be done, which items are best done at the same time and where costs can be cut. I normally find that the repair, structural, plumbing and electrical elements are the most difficult to alter, as they are specialised jobs and there aren't usually many obvious economies. But with fittings, decorations and sometimes joinery you could:

- Opt to provide the units, lights, kitchen appliances, sanitary ware, etc. yourself and just pay the builder for the labour. Do check that you can actually get the items for less than he has provided for (he should have indicated a PC – prime cost – sum for this in his spec) and take into account the organisational aspect of getting the right fittings to him at the appropriate time. Any delay will be your responsibility and so will be the time he stands doing nothing. If you can fit in a bit of running around, you can save quite a packet (enough for that extended stay in the health farm you'll be needing).

- Go in for a bit of DIY; if there is any chance of your wielding a paintbrush do consider taking over the decorations. I have to admit that there is nothing quite like a professional paint job (lovely smooth, eggshell thin, rock hard coats of paint), but if money is a problem it is much more important that the repairs get done, and most people can make a very decent stab at painting when they try! You could even ask the builder to quote to preparation level, i.e. he does the hard work of rubbing down, sugar soaping, etc., and you then just apply the paint.

■ Try to come up with some clever alternatives. Never forget that a builder will only quote you on what you have asked for, which is not necessarily the best or most complete solution – in other words, he is not liable to think outside your brief, so don't expect him to. You, on the other hand, have a vested interest in being ingenious. For example:

– Don't be persuaded that a non-standard-sized kitchen needs to be hand built; standard units can be cut down.
– Alternate tiled areas with plain painted or wallpapered areas. Tiles are expensive both to buy and apply, and in bathrooms/kitchens are really only of practical use where they cover an area which is likely to get splashed and need wiping.
– In awkward-sized bathrooms see if you can avoid the need for built in vanity units. Go for a cheaper, freestanding basin instead and then find the lost storage space in a wall cupboard; conversely, a bit of panelling around a cheap bath can look just as good as one of those cast iron Victorian jobs.

The gist of all this is that you have to keep paring down until the spec fits the budget (go back to Chapter One), but this doesn't necessarily mean denying yourself every last wish. Having got the price pretty much where you want it, your final task is to award the tender to one party. Many people automatically opt for the very cheapest quotation, but your final choice should be influenced by a combination of factors, namely:

■ your reaction to the builder – do you like and trust him?
■ his track record – has he done good work in the past?
■ your confidence in his ability to finish on time.
■ his enthusiasm for the project – is he likely to put quality and spirit into the work?
■ oh yes, and the price . . .

When you have made a choice, confirm acceptance to the builder in writing. You should also write to those who have been rejected, partly to tie up loose ends and partly as a courtesy. Unless you really feel it would be helpful to tell the builder exactly why he didn't get the job (e.g. for reasons of price, proximity etc.), a short and simple letter will suffice – something along the lines of:

Dear Mr Smith,

Thankyou very much for quoting for the refurbishment of 22 Jones Street.

I have now compared all three quotations but after much consideration have opted for one of the others. I hope that you will not be too disappointed. Once again, thankyou for your tender.

Yours sincerely,

J Black

John Black.

THE CONTRACT

Alongside the specification you should have a document laying out the terms of your agreement. This can be anything from a short letter to a 30-page contract, depending on the scale of the job and your personal preference. Even if you don't have either of these, simply making a verbal agreement with a builder constitutes a contract in the eyes of the law – but of course any disputes are that much more difficult to sort out because there is no proof of what was agreed. You are therefore strongly advised to have something in writing. If you do choose to make use of a contract, mention this to the builder before he spends time working on the specification; it is only fair to allow him to see the contract terms and agree them in principle before going to the trouble of preparing a specification. Otherwise, not only has he wasted his time, but you haven't got a deal either! The options are as follows:

JCT Minor Works Contract
One of the contracts drawn up by industry bodies, e.g. JCT Minor Works 1980. The JCT is a very long document and might well frighten

off many smaller builders. It is very thorough and undoubtedly good practice, but in the real world is not always used, mainly because of its complexity. Architects and building surveyors are familiar with its contents and may well suggest it as a client/builder contract, but if you are managing the builder yourself and are uncomfortable with all the detail, it might be as well to go for something less formal.

At the time of writing the BEC were just putting the finishing touches to a Form for Smaller Works (where no architect is engaged), specifically devised for jobs where the client may use an architect or surveyor only for drawing up plans, and then manage the builder himself, i.e. an agreement directly between the client and builder (unlike the JCT forms which all envisage the use of an architect throughout). The form is short, simple, user friendly and available from the BEC publications department. Only about four pages long, it covers all the details of starting dates, variations in work, payment, insurance, disputes, etc. In short, it looks as if it will fill a long-standing gap in the contracts market.

A 'homemade' contract

Some builders, especially if they are a smallish business, will undoubtedly run a mile from contracts such as those above. This is where a less intimidating document can play its part. You have to strike a balance between what is comprehensive and technically correct but not too laborious – it's not easy but the example below covers most eventualities. You may want to add to it or simplify further. Either way, if you are making use of a 'homemade contract', get the final version looked over by a solicitor before signing.

SPECIMEN 'HOMEMADE' CONTRACT

1. Between ....(the employer) of ....

and .... (the contractor) ....

2. The contractor shall carry out the work described in the attached specification in a good and workmanlike manner for the fixed sum of £................. plus VAT at the standard rate.

3. The employer shall remove all furniture, fixtures and fittings necesary for the contractor to carry out the work.

4. The work shall commence on .... and be completed by .... Hours of work will be 9am–5pm, with the usual allowances for lunch and tea breaks.

5. Time is of the essence with regard to this work. The completion date will only be extended if factors outside the control of the contractor prevent the work being completed on time. If the contractor leaves the site for more than 5 consecutive days, without reasonable explanation, the employer may terminate the contract.

6. The contractor shall provide all labour, materials and equipment necessary to carry out the work, unless otherwise stipulated in writing by the employer.

7. Unless otherwise specified, all materials should be new and fit for their purpose.

8. The contractor shall not remove any materials or fittings from site unless given written permission to do so by the employer.

9. The employer shall provide all necessary services and facilities (provided adequate notice is given by the contractor).

10. The contractor/employer (delete as applicable) shall make application for planning permission and building regulations approval as necessary. The contractor/employer (delete as applicable) shall make all notifications and arrange inspections in connection with the work.

11. The contractor is at all times fully responsible for his subcontractors.

12. The contractor shall be responsible at all times for making the site safe and secure.

13. Any variations to the work detailed in the specification (and time/costing thereof) must be agreed in writing before being carried out.

14. The contractor shall take full responsibility for the works and make good at his own expense any loss or damage caused either by himself or his subcontractors.

15. The contractor shall insure against any loss arising from his activities and agree to show his insurance policy to the employer upon request.

16. The contractor shall maintain a tidy site while work is in progress, removing rubbish on a daily or weekly basis as necessary. Upon completion of the work, the site will be left clean and tidy and all debris removed.

17. The contractor shall not assign any part of the contract without the written permission of the employer.

18. The employer shall pay the contractor on a monthly basis, upon presentation of an invoice, against works specified and completed to the complete satisfaction of the employer.

19. The employer shall withhold ......% of the final payment for a period of six months from completion of the work, in case of defects arising from workmanship or materials used. In the event of this amount being insufficient to cover such defects, the contractor shall make good at his own expense.

Signed .... (the employer)

Signed ....(the contractor)

Date ....

Key

1. Always include the full name and address of both parties. If the builder is a limited company, state his registered address.

2. You may need to delete the sentence on VAT, depending upon whether or not your builder is registered for it. You may also have to allow for the fact that some parts of the spec are only estimates and have to be sanctioned (in writing) as work progresses.

3. The property may be fully furnished, in which case you will have to agree the condition it should be in for the builder to start work. At the very least he will need it cleared of all freestanding furniture and you will probably want to organise that yourself, especially if there are expensive or valued items to be moved.

4 & 5. You have to be reasonable and accept that bad weather or sudden illness are outside the builder's control. On the other hand, you want to be able to terminate the contract if he is trying to do three jobs at once and making you wait in the process. Unless you are only having small works done or are lucky enough to have somewhere else to live, you may be renting a property while the work takes place. A significant delay could put a large dent in your budget, not to mention the inconvenience of being unable to resume a normal life. If you do have to cancel the contract and get someone else to do the work, you can claim from the original builder any costs involved in doing so.

6. This is a 'catch all' phrase to protect you from little extras slipping in. You must stipulate when, if at all, you want to provide the building materials yourself; for instance, tiles for a bathroom or special flagstones for a kitchen floor. But think carefully about this because you will be the one who has to get the goods on site, take them back if they are faulty and accept the loss if something happens in transit. It may be better to tell the builder exactly what you want and where to get it, then let him do the rest. The cost will be a very small part of your overall budget and may even be offset if the builder gets a trade discount and passes it on to you. It isn't always cost effective to do the work yourself.

7 & 8 It is not unknown for builders to try to use secondhand materials yet charge for the item as new, hence this clause – although occasionally you may want old materials, e.g. slates or timbers. What's more, you don't want anything removed from site without your permission; I know of one couple who asked for their floor to be relaid, meaning that they wanted the existing York flagstones repositioned. The builder misinterpreted the instructions, removed the very valuable York stones, sold them and put cheap imitations in their place. Be warned.

9. A tricky one this. I feel that in the spirit of co-operation the 'employer' should provide adequate power, light and water (and telephone if necessary) to allow the builder to get the job done. In addition, you should give the workers somewhere to make tea, shelter in case of rain, and use of a loo. However, this can be abused; it is not unheard of for builders to deliberately block the loo with their morning newspaper and then use that as an excuse for being late – it being your responsibility for unblocking it! I jest not. You may want to turn this clause around and make it the builder's responsibility to provide all services and facilities – indeed some do have their own generators and portaloos. It pretty much boils down to the level of trust between both of you.

10. It is very important to establish who is responsible for both the initial application and subsequent checks. Failure to do this could result in delays, work having to be redone and at the very worst, prosecution and fines. This clause also covers things such as utilities, etc.

11. Another very important clause. Your contract is with the builder and it is his responsibility to make sure that the work done is in accordance with the terms of your contract, whether that work is carried out by himself or a subcontractor. The advantage to you is that in the event of a dispute, you only have one person to pursue! The only circumstances under which you might have a separate agreement with the subcontractor is if he or she is responsible for a design element, e.g. of a kitchen. Make sure you know whom your contract is with.

12. Don't think that this is just fine detail and can be dispensed with; I know someone whose builder decided to remove a glass door from its frame and then before leaving for the day, stood it back, unattached, in the doorway. The result was that my friend later went to 'open' the door and fell with it as it crashed to the ground, injuring his hand in the process. Unfortunately he had nothing in writing about safety on site.

13. The words 'in writing' are crucial here. You will probably cover a lot of things when in conversation with the builder, and you must have a golden rule that only points which are confirmed in writing can be acted upon – otherwise, if anything goes wrong, it will be down to you to prove that you didn't give the verbal go ahead, and that can be very tricky.

14. This of course refers to losses that do not constitute part of the agreed works, e.g. knocking down a wall to create a through lounge might be part of your agreement, whereas a wall collapsing due to the builder's negligence obviously would not.

15. It is quite common to ask to see a copy of the builder's insurance. After all, if you don't and it is inadequate, or non-existent, the immediate burden of repair, etc. will fall to you. Check to see if it includes third party insurance, in case of injury or loss to your neighbours, etc. And don't forget to inform your own insurance company of exactly what work is planned and any subsequent changes to that plan, particularly if the house is likely to be less secure as a result of the work, e.g. no glass in the windows, roof tiles missing.

16. This applies both to the obvious rubbish and the stuff which builders often try to hide away, e.g. by sweeping it behind the foot boards of new kitchen units rather than taking it outside!

17. Know that if he has a better opportunity elsewhere, a builder may well try to get someone else to do part of your job for him, which could have disastrous consequences. This clause protects you against people being brought in without your knowledge and permission – something which can easily happen if you are not living on site.

18. If the job is a small one you may want to amend this clause and pay in one go at the end of the job. Otherwise, staged payments are a very good idea, because you are being much more specific about exactly what you are paying for and the phrase 'complete satisfaction' allows you to withhold money should the work not be up to scratch (see Chapter Eight); but you in turn mustn't use it as a tool to extract unfair discounts, etc. Don't be surprised if the builder requests some form of proof that you can actually pay for the work you are commissioning — yes, it works both ways! It has been known for people to get totally carried away with their specification, be unable to pay for completed work or to call a halt halfway through when the builder has already bought materials or engaged subcontractors. Typically, you might be asked to provide evidence from your bank that the money is available or even to set it aside in a special bank or building society account. I certainly wouldn't allow anyone other than yourself access to these accounts, but I do think it reasonable for you to demonstrate your ability to pay for the work, especially on a large job.

19. This is fairly standard practice in building work and in the recent recession builders have accepted defects periods as long as twelve months, but the norm is six months and 5 – 10 per cent. Bear in mind that the clause only relates to defects in the workmanship or the materials used, but not necessarily to items such as shrinkage, which often occurs regardless of the quality of the work. Remember that if the builder will not put right any defects, you are within your rights to get another builder to finish the job and to set the cost of that work against the first builder's invoice.

A simple letter of agreement

This may be perfectly adequate if you are just having a bit of remedial work/decorating done, but remember that what you don't say can be as important as what you do; in other words, accept that this cannot be completely comprehensive and relies upon a certain amount of trust and goodwill. (See the example on p. 66.)

In return, you may find that some builders have their own terms and conditions which you are required to sign. If so, remember the following:

- Always read all the small print before signing anything.
- Take your time and don't be rushed, if there is anything you don't understand or don't agree with, ask for it to be crossed out and countersigned, or better still, retyped.
- Always get a copy of anything you have signed and do not give your go ahead until you have received copies of all relevant paperwork.
- Regardless of what is said in a contract, your statutory rights cannot be taken away. Indeed, if any clauses are unfair, they will be rendered invalid under the Unfair Contract Terms Act 1977.

Lastly, if you want ultimate control over the builder, insist upon a rolling contract; this effectively says that the contract is only valid for one task or groups of tasks at a time, and is only carried over to the next if you are satisfied with the previous one. The idea is that it keeps the pressure on the builder, and according to people who have used it, works very effectively. I am not quite so sure – a contract can make provision for most things but, as far as I am concerned, there is absolutely no substitute for communication. You will get a lot more out of your builder through reasoned discussion than by holding him on a leash so tight he can't function.

I hope you are still feeling bushy-tailed, because now we get technical.

Figure 6. Specimen letter of agreement

5 Monks Road
Colham
Darkshire

21 June 1994

Mr Dirk
Buildco Ltd
28 Bint Street
Colham

Dear Mr Dirk,

Thank you for your quotation for renovation works to be carried out on my house.

I confirm acceptance of your quotation subject to the following:

1. That the price quoted is a firm one. Any changes to the nature and cost of the work to be agreed in writing before being implemented.
2. That the work should start on 28 July 1994 and be finished by 20 September 1994.
3. That all work will be carried out by yourself unless otherwise agreed in writing.
4. That you take full responsibility for any damage caused to my property during renovation works.
5. That you keep the site safe, secure and tidy at all times.

I agree to pay you weekly against works completed. The final payment to be made when all works have been completed to my satisfaction.

Yours sincerely

J Worth

Mr John Worth

CHAPTER FOUR

Playing by the Rules

'Little things are infinitely the most important'
(*Sir Arthur Conan Doyle*)

You should by now have a clear idea of how you want your property to look after renovation and what professional help you will need to achieve this. You will most likely have fallen into a sort of halfway house, whereby you have decided to engage a professional for any designs or plans, but want to organise the builder yourself – usually for reasons of cost. This is perfectly feasible, but means that the onus of seeking any appropriate official permissions needed to proceed with this work, namely planning permission and building regulations approval, falls to you (or your builder if that is part of your agreement). People often confuse these two processes (often quite conveniently, according to the planning officers) but they are completely separate. So never assume that planning permission gives you building regulations approval or vice versa. Each requires a separate application and in any property renovation, either one or both *may* be relevant and can take several months to process; you should therefore seek your builder's advice as to whether they will be necessary as soon as you start discussing the spec. Alternatively, go straight to your local planning and building departments for their advice. At the same time you should be giving some thought to your utility requirements.

And just before we begin, I have decided not to apologise for the detail you are about to be subjected to. Just bear in mind that the following is but a summary (!) and you really do have to come to grips with the detail if you want to make the applications yourself.

The key to success

In a word, Tactics. Before you get into the technical details, understand how to approach the planning and building officers and you are already some of the way towards success. Most applicants view them as small, power-mad individuals out to make life difficult. The relationship is confrontational from the start. Actually, they are just doing their job, the spirit of which is to encourage building – providing it is sensible and safe. The secret is to make the first move; go and speak to the relevant officers before you put pen to paper. They are all human, nay, open to flattery, and probably keen to help. So if in doubt, ask.

Don't be put off from making the application yourself and don't necessarily believe an architect/surveyor/builder, etc. who suggests that they have connections which can sway the outcome. It's just more business for them and as the person who owns the property, you should want to be involved with making the application. Buildings are actually quite simple things and there is no reason why you shouldn't manage most of the paperwork yourself, although it is important to make sure that any application is supported by adequate plans and calculations – which will probably have to be provided by a professional. If you do give the job to anyone else, make sure that their responsibility for compliance is written into your contract with them and that you see all relevant correspondence.

PLANNING PERMISSION

What it means

In simple terms, the Town and Country Planning Act 1990 (which defines the purpose and nature of planning control) is all about regulating how our land is used and examining how any proposed work is likely to affect the general character of an area. In particular with property renovations it will assess the effect of this work on the character and appearance of the building itself, of the area around it and of neighbouring properties. The Planning Act is controlled nationally and determined in Parliament (the Scottish system differs slightly), but its interpretation is left to each local planning authority and can therefore vary slightly from place to place.

When it is necessary

Always remember that the concept of planning is essentially a positive one, i.e. that you should be able to do sensible and minor works to your property without having to seek permission. To that end, you can repair and maintain a property without planning permission provided that you don't materially affect the external appearance and character of the building. Many property renovations are largely a question of internal updating and may thus be exempt. But it will be regarded as a form of development and necessitate planning permission if you want to:

- extend;
- rebuild;
- institute a change of use (e.g. splitting a house into flats); or
- materially affect the external appearance of the building.

When it is not

There are, however, exceptions to this rule, which are laid out in Part One of The General Development Order 1988 ('development within the curtilage of a dwelling house'); in simple language, you can extend your house (this does not include flats) by a limited amount without planning permission – 70 cubic metres (2,471 cubic feet) or 15 per cent of the volume of the house. This is reduced to 50 cubic metres if you live in a conservation area, an Area of Outstanding Natural Beauty (AONB), a National Park or a terraced house. But this is a 'one off' allowance and if the previous owner/occupier had already used the quota and you subsequently wanted to do more work, further planning permission would be required.

Listed buildings and conservation areas

Special mention should be made of listed buildings and conservation areas. For the former you would need Listed Building Consent to alter the property in any way at all – either internally or externally, e.g. for a new staircase, to remove panelling, etc. It is an offence to carry out works to a listed building without the necessary consent. Within a conservation area you need permission to demolish any part of a building which is larger than 115 cubic metres (4,060 cubic feet). This

Figure 7.

PLANNING
APPLICATION
FORM
Town & Country Planning Act 1990

Please read accompanying notes before answering any questions. Complete all sections in BLOCK CAPITALS and answer every question. Four copies of the completed form and six sets of drawings as specified in Note 5 are required.

I apply for planning permission and declare that to the best of my knowledge all the information contained in this application form and on submitted plans is correct.

SIGNED _____ **Applicant/Agent.**
(Please delete)

DATED _____

FEE (Please delete/insert as appropriate)
– I enclose the application fee of £ _____
– No fee is payable for the following reason: _____

by cheque/P.O. No. _____

For Office use only:
UPRN
RN
Fee Req'd.: £ _____ : Paid £ _____
Owing : £ _____ : Cheque/PO

Applicant (If any) to whom correspondence will be sent

Name: _____

Address: _____

_____ Post Code: _____

Tel No: _____

Contact Name/Ref.: _____

1 Applicant

Name: _____

Address: _____

_____ Post Code: _____

Tel No: _____

2 Address of Application Site

Postcode _____

Does this include listed buildings/structures?   Yes ☐   No ☐

3 Description of Proposed Development

_____
_____

4 Type of Application (Tick as appropriate)

A ☐ A full application for new building works and/or change of use.

B ☐ An outline application - Please tick those matters for which approval is sought at this stage.

    Siting ☐   Access ☐   Design ☐   External Appearance ☐   Landscaping ☐

C ☐ An application for removal/alteration of a condition of a previous planning permission.

D ☐ An application for renewal of a permission.

E ☐ An application for buildings or works already carried out or use of land already started.

    Date of completion of works or when change of use occurred ☐

- If you have ticked C or D, please give date ☐ of previous permission and our reference [RN] ☐

5 Plans and drawings Submitted with this Application

Please list all drawings, plans and documents forming part of this application which should have distinctive reference numbers:

_____
_____

Please specify type and colour of external materials here (or in a covering letter) and on your plans.

_____

71

ruling also applies to walls, which, if they are adjoining a highway, are more than 1 metre (3 ft 3 inches) in height; if not adjoining a highway, they need to be more than 2 metres (6½ feet) in height before you need consent. You will also find that design controls are stricter in conservation areas and will be scrutinised particularly for their aesthetic qualities. If you are reading this book before buying a property I would strongly advise you to check if the house has Listed Building Status and to obtain the necessary permissions before exchanging contracts.

If in doubt – ask

You can no doubt see from the above summary that there is plenty of room for error if you make an uninformed decision on whether or not planning permission is necessary. So the short answer is to go and discuss your proposals with the local planning department before you put in an application. They can tell you straightaway whether or not planning approval is required (and what has been done in the past). If it is, and you are deciding on the design details yourself, they can advise on technical aspects, e.g. the correct proportion of windows, all of which can save delays at a later stage and ensure that once the application is submitted, it can be determined promptly. There is even now a Citizens' Charter Guide, available from your local authority, which lays out the standards of service you can expect from the council when using the planning system – they really do appear to be trying!

How to make an application

The various stages are as follows:

1. To get your proposals drawn up in a format which is clear and acceptable to the planning office. Unless you are confident and competent enough to draw the plans yourself, always employ a surveyor/architect/architectural technician to do this on your behalf. You can still submit the drawings and shepherd them through the application process, but you will have made sure that they are presented in the required professional format.

2. To complete the Planning Application Form (see Figure 7). Most local planning authorities issue guidance notes for making a planning application. These explain very clearly what information you have to provide, and in the case of renovation works it is basically:

Figure 8. Location Plan

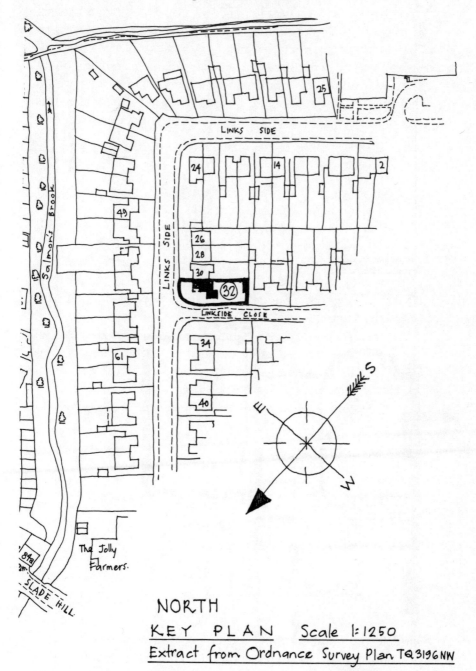

LINKS SIDE

LINKS SIDE

LINKFIDE CLOSE

25

24   14   2

49

26
28
30
32

34

61

40

The Jolly Farmers.

SLADE HILL

N   S   E   W

NORTH

KEY PLAN   Scale 1:1250

Extract from Ordnance Survey Plan TQ3196NW

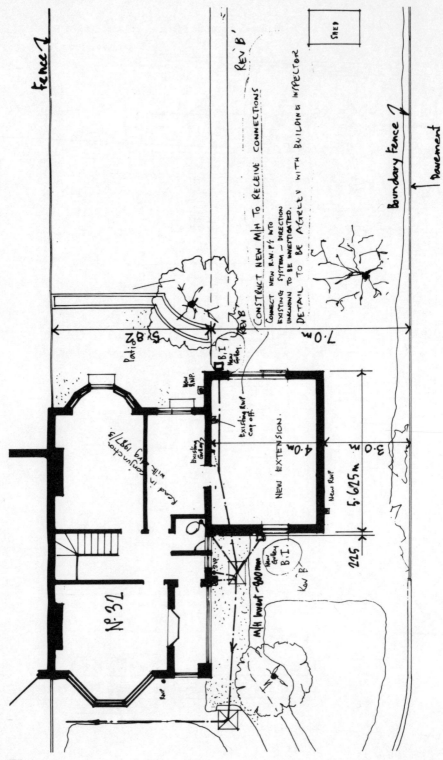

Fig. 9. Drawings Showing Elevations and (opposite) part of the Site Plan

Lintols
← CN 18 1·2 m long

← CN 18 1·2 m long

FRONT   ELEVATION

SIDE   ELEVATION

Lintols
CN 19 (B) →
2·55 long

CN 20 2·55 long →

REAR   ELEVATION

- a location plan showing exactly where the site is. You can use an OS map with a scale of either 1:2500 or 1:1250 (see Figure 8);
- accurate drawings (1:100 scale), showing elevations and plans both existing and proposed, which demonstrate fully and clearly what you are applying for (see Figure 9);
- details of materials to be used (for extensions and alterations), in particular for the external finish and appearance;
- details relating to access, refuse storage, parking, means of escape from fire and any proposed felling of trees;
- a certificate of land ownership.

In addition, if you have a listed building or are in a conservation area, you will also have to submit an application for Listed Building Consent or Conservation Area Consent respectively. If in doubt about any aspect of the form(s), consult your planning officer before submitting the application; any proposals which are incomplete or invalid will not be accepted.

3. To submit the form and plans, together with the appropriate planning fee.

4. To wait for an acknowledgement of receipt from the local authority. If for any reason you have not given enough information they will come back for more detail, e.g. materials specification.

5. To inform your neighbours of your proposed works. Local authorities will either advertise receipt of your application in the local newspaper or consult anyone likely to be affected, such as your neighbour (they have a duty to give 'adequate notice' of your proposals). But it obviously makes sense for you to speak to your neighbour before they do, and involve him or her in the decision-making process from the beginning.

6. To wait for a decision. In theory this should take no longer than eight weeks, but in practice can take longer and will either be a straightforward approval, an approval with conditions or a refusal with reasons. Take heart from the fact that about 85 per cent of applications are approved.

What to do if your application is turned down

If your application is refused you have the right of appeal. The necessary forms are available from the Department of the Environment or, in Wales, the Planning Inspectorate of the Welsh Office. (Scotland and Northern Ireland have their own system.) There are three methods of appeal:

1. A public inquiry, usually reserved for large-scale plans, e.g. supermarket developments, and involving phalanxes of legal representatives at huge cost.

2. An informal hearing at which both you and the local authority present your case to a planning inspector, who then decides.

3. Written representations, whereby both you and the local authority submit written statements, the planning inspector then visits the site and adjudicates. This is the normal procedure for smaller applications.

This time the balance goes in favour of the local authority; as a national average, only about a third of appeals are won by the applicant.

What happens if you carry out works without permission

Having read this chapter there is no excuse for going ahead with works before appropriate planning permission has been granted. You simply run the risk of either your neighbour or the local authority noticing and making further enquiries. Sometimes, however, because of time constraints or bad weather, people are tempted to go ahead regardless. Be warned that the planning office does have wide-ranging powers, which are as follows:

An enforcement notice
This could, for example, require you to demolish an extension built without permission because it adversely affects the character of the area. In other words, you can be made to remove any unauthorised development *and* restore the property to its original state.

A stop notice

If work is still in progress, a stop notice (which is issued in association with an enforcement notice) can halt the procedure completely after three days and prevent any further work. It is a criminal offence to continue work once this notice has been issued.

Of course, there are ways to abuse the system; people apply to appeal through the Secretary of State, delay the hearing, say they will voluntarily stop work and then carry on. But considering that two-thirds of appeals go in favour of the authority, this would seem to be a high-risk strategy.

What happens if you don't carry out planning permission properly

It is one thing to go ahead without planning permission, but once granted, it must be carried out properly; this is partly so that the end result is safe for all concerned, but also because you will want to obtain a certificate of completion for the work (which will be helpful when you are selling the property) and to do that the Planning Officer will have to come and inspect what you have done. If the work is inadequate you can be served with a Breach of Condition Notice, to which there is no appeal. Failure to comply can land you in court.

BUILDING REGULATIONS

What are they?

They are a set of controls designed to regulate the technical aspects of building and quality of construction and workmanship. Whereas planning permission decides whether or not certain works can take place at all, building regulations come into effect when building work begins. They aim to ensure that acceptable standards of 'Health, Safety, Welfare and Energy Conservation' are met and adhered to – in other words, that people have adequate sanitation, safe heating appliances, means of escape in a fire, and so on. Their scope is pretty wide-ranging and it's fair to say that the majority of medium- to large-scale renovations will be affected by them.

As with planning regulations, they are determined in Parliament and applied by the local authority (the specific department is normally called Building Control although in London this work is carried out by the District Surveyor). Given that there are some 450 local authorities in the UK, there can occasionally be regional variation in the way that building regulations are applied. But the source documents are The Building Act 1984, The Building Regulations 1991, various other Local Acts and within London, The London Building Acts (Amendment) Act 1939 as well. Once again, Scotland and Northern Ireland have their own system.

When do they apply?

Remember that building regulations are not dependent on planning permission. Even if the latter isn't required, building regulations can still come into force. The following works (all of which could apply in property renovation) come under 'Building Regs' control:

- The erection or extension of a building.
- The provision of a controlled service or fitting e.g. the provision of hot and cold water and the drainage of it from WCs, baths and basins, and the provision of fires and boilers (which strictly speaking, covers the installation of items such as a gas fire or new boiler).
- The material alteration of a building, or a controlled service, e.g. gas fire, or fitting e.g. cooker. (N.B. In reality you might be hard pressed to get a Building Inspector to come out and check a simple replacement of e.g. a heating appliance or cooker but remember that any work with gas appliances **must** be carried out by a Corgi registered gas installer.)
- Work required to be undertaken as a result of a material change of use, e.g. a barn conversion or subdivision of a property into flats.
- The insertion of insulation material into the cavity wall of a building.
- Work involving the underpinning of a building or any other structural alterations.

If you live in London there are a few extra conditions under the London Building Acts 1930–9 likely to apply to renovation work. They can be found in sections 21, 35 and 138, and refer to openings in party walls, means of escape in flats more than 2 storeys high and the demolition of external and party walls.

And when don't they?

Some buildings and works, however, are exempt:

- Small detached buildings under 30 sq metres (323 sq feet) in floor area where no sleeping accommodation is provided, e.g. a garage.
- The extension of a building by the addition at ground level of a conservatory, canopy, porch, covered way or carport, providing the floor area does not exceed 30 sq metres (323 sq feet), and satisfies safety glazing requirements.

However, the real thrust of building regs is that:

- For all new construction work (or that which implements a change of use), the technical requirements of the regulations apply in full.

- If you are just carrying out alterations (internal or external), your only obligation is to demonstrate that the work has left the property no worse off than before and preferably in better condition. But . . . don't start leaping around in the false belief that you fall into this category and can get away with doing nothing. Building requirements are complex and even in my following brief summary of their content (and I mean just a summary), you will see how they can suddenly become relevant when you are least expecting it.

The technical requirements

The legal and technical requirements of the regulations and guidance on how to meet those requirements are contained in what are called 'Approved Documents A-N' (published by the Department of the Environment and on sale from HMSO or they can be referred to at your local authority and many libraries). The official line is that you don't have to follow these recommendations to the letter, so long as you can demonstrate compliance with the regulations overall. If you do follow them, however, this will be seen as 'evidence tending to show' that you have complied with the regulations. Convoluted, isn't it? What they are really saying is that they cannot force people to use the documents for guidance, but prefer them to because it helps set common standards and procedures – and that does have some logic! In any event, the Approved Documents represent the cheapest means of complying and are therefore to be recommended. In summary, they are as follows:

Summary of Approved Documents A-N

A. *Structure:* e.g. that the building should contain correct sizes of structural elements, e.g. of lintels to ensure stability.

B. *Fire Safety:* e.g. that people should be able to escape 'unaided, to a place of safety'. For example, you might be contemplating a loft conversion and deem this an 'alteration'. However, by creating another storey to the property you would then have to ensure an adequate means of escape in case of fire. NB. Building Regs people are particularly hot on A and B.

C. *Site preparation and resistance to moisture:* e.g. that the ground covered by a building should be free from growths and contaminants, and the building itself be resistant to moisture leaking in.

D. *Toxic substances:* e.g. that fumes from cavity wall insulation must be prevented from permeating into occupied buildings.

E. *Resistance to the passage of sound:* e.g. between walls and floors which separate a dwelling from another building or dwelling.

F. *Ventilation:* e.g. that there should be adequate means of ventilation in the building, especially for roof voids, sanitary accommodation and bathrooms. Living rooms and bedrooms are supposed to have an openable window of 1 sq metre (10.76 sq feet) for every 20 sq metres (215.2 sq feet) of room space – although this rule may be relaxed for some buildings, e.g. for listed buildings.

G. *Hygiene:* e.g. that dwellings should have a bathroom or shower room with bath and hot and cold water. If you simply wanted to alter the position of e.g. a WC, approval would not necessarily be required, but it would (see H), if the work involved new, or an extension of existing, drainage or plumbing.

H. *Drainage and waste disposal:* e.g. that adequate systems of foul water and surface water drainage must be provided. This could become relevant if you were, for example, converting a barn to a dwelling – in that instance all work would have to comply fully with regulations because there wouldn't be any existing amenities.

J. *Heat-producing appliances:* e.g. that any new appliances should have adequate ventilation for the appliance to function and that the fabric of the building is not put at risk from fire.

K. *Stairs, ramps and guards:* e.g. that they must afford safe passage and be adequately guarded. Ideally, these should be at no more than a 42 degree angle. There are also specific dimensions for the step and tread and a 2-metre headroom allowance. Obviously, this can present a few problems in an older property, but it should none the less be discussed with the building control department.

L. *Conservation of fuel and power:* e.g. that adequate provision be made for the conservation of fuel and power in buildings, such as by having adequate insulation.

M. *Access and facilities for disabled people:* (not applicable for dwelling houses).

N. *Glazing – materials and protection:* e.g. that all new doors and full-height windows have suitable approved safety glazing (e.g. to BSI standard).

Potentially, all of these could apply in domestic property renovation, except perhaps D and M. In other words, if in any doubt as to which building regs you need to comply with – ask!

Setting standards

You can take it as read that some builders (especially cowboys) will view building regulations as a minimum standard that they are forced, grudgingly, to meet, and will fall short of wherever possible. Common sense tells you, however, that it is in your interests to exceed these minimum standards wherever possible, especially with items such as thermal insulation. You can control this without creating bad feeling. Tell the builder at the beginning of the job that you are going to meet regularly with the building inspector on site, or at least be present when the inspector meets the builder. You can always supplement this with a private meeting back at the inspector's office. The builder is far less likely to skip on the detail with two pairs of eyes on him and you may find the building inspector turns out to be a real unpaid ally!

How to make an application

You can make one of two types of application:

1. Building Notice Approval

This method is really suitable for people carrying out small building works such as a straightforward domestic extension, the formation of new simple structural openings, installation of a heating appliance, etc., the idea being that if the work is straightforward, it should be subject to fewer regulations and allowed to proceed more quickly. In fact you are not even given any sort of formal 'go ahead' and only have to give notification to the local authority 48 hours before work starts. You simply fill in a Building Notice Approval form (see Figure 10). This requires only basic information about yourself and the work you want to do:

- Your name and address (and that of any agent working on your behalf);
- A statement that the building notice procedure is being used;
- Description of the work;
- Location;
- Use of the building;
- Number of storeys;
- Drainage particulars;

and further details of cavity wall insulation or unvented hot water system installation (if applicable), together with a set of simple plans, which are often planning drawings (see Figure 10) with notes. A site inspector then calls when work commences and determines whether or not you have complied with regulations. If so, all well and good, but if you have used this route to avoid compliance with the regulations and the work isn't up to standard, the site inspector can take you back to square one with the potential for enforcement action. Be prepared, because the council can ask for plans and details to be submitted once work has started, e.g. calculations for steel beams. Ask the inspector before works whether further detail will be requested.

2. Full Plans Approval

In this instance you seek approval before work starts, usually because the nature of the work is more complex. The application (see Figure 11) is much more detailed than that for Building Notice Approval and

Figure 10.

MONMOUTH BOROUGH COUNCIL
CYNGOR BWRDEISTREF MYNWY

Mamhilad House
Mamhilad Park Estate
Pontypool
Gwent NP4 0YL

TEL: (0495) 762311
FAX: (0495) 762329

BUILDING
NOTICE
The Building Act 1984
The Building Regulations 1991

Building Regulations
Plan Number:

This form is to be filled in by the person who intends to carry out building work or agent. If the form is unfamiliar please read the notes on the reverse side or consult the office indicated above. Please type or use block capitals.

1 Applicant's details (see note 1)
Name:
Address:
Postcode: Tel: Fax:

2 Agent's details (if applicable)
Name:
Address:
Postcode: Tel: Fax:

3 Location of building to which work relates
Address:
Postcode: Tel: Fax:

4 Proposed work
Number of storeys:
Description:

Date of commencement (if known, see note 6):

5 Use of building
1 If new building or extension please state proposed use:
2 If existing building state present use:

6 Fees (see note 8 and separate Guidance Note on Fees for information)
1 If Schedule 1 work please state number of dwellings with floor area under 64m^2:   , over 64m^2:
2 If Schedule 2 work please state floor area: m^2
3 If Schedule 3 work please state the estimated cost of work excluding VAT: £
Building notice fee: £   plus VAT: £   Total: £

7 Statement
This notice is given in relation to the building work as described, and is submitted in accordance with Regulation 11(1)(a).

Name: Signature: Date:

must show all constructional details, i.e. plans, sections, elevations, and their compliance with the requirements of the regulations (see Figure 12). The site inspector then merely checks that the work has been carried out in line with the approved plans. The advantage of this prior approval is that it ensures virtual immunity from any enforcement action (providing, of course, you have built to these approved plans), simply because the inspector cannot really come back and say that something is not acceptable after it has been officially sanctioned. You also get the benefit of free advice on design, layout, structural elements, fire precautions, energy conservation and sound transmission – all there for the asking. Anybody purchasing a property with a view to renovation may well find that their Building Society requires evidence of Full Plans Approval. A Full Plans Application has to be submitted with two full sets of plans and a plan fee.

For both Building Notice and Full Plans Approval your application should be accompanied by any relevant drawings, specifications and/or calculations necessary to demonstrate compliance with safety requirements on the structure of the building. Failure to do so will only delay your application, as the local authority will want them, whatever the type of application. Unless you have the appropriate knowledge of building construction this should be done by a professional, i.e. an architect, structural engineer or building surveyor. Figure 12 is a detail from a full set of plans. Full plans would include drawings of all elevations.

Remember to ask for advice

Do consider approaching your building regulations inspectorate before deciding which type of application to go for. They may well be able to save you a lot of work by indicating which building regs are relevant and how much detailed preparation they want to see. For example, if you were organising a simple alteration such as a through lounge, they might be satisfied with an informal agreement as to how this work would be done. On the other hand, for something more complicated, like a back extension, they would almost certainly require detailed plans. Until a few years ago notices and full plans were required on all building regulation applications. But there is now a degree of support for sensible, informal agreements whenever possible. In other words, it could be greatly to your advantage to speak to the building regulations inspector before you start submitting any applications.

Figure 11.

MONMOUTH BOROUGH COUNCIL
CYNGOR BWRDEISTREF MYNWY

Mamhilad House
Mamhilad Park Estate
Pontypool
Gwent NP4 0YL

TEL: (0495) 762311
FAX: (0495) 762329

FULL PLANS
SUBMISSION

The Building Act 1984
The Building Regulations 1991

Building Regulations
Plan Number:

This form is to be filled in by the person who intends to carry out building work or agent. If the form is unfamiliar please read the notes on the reverse side or consult the office indicated above. Please type or use block capitals.

1 Applicant's details (see note 1)
Name:
Address:
Postcode: Tel: Fax:

2 Agent's details (if applicable)
Name:
Address:
Postcode: Tel: Fax:

3 Location of building to which work relates
Address:
Postcode: Tel: Fax:

4 Proposed work
Description:

5 Use of building
1 If new building or extension please state proposed use:
2 If existing building state present use:
3 Is the building to be put, or intended to be put, to a use which is
designated for the purpose of the Fire Precautions Act 1971 (see note 5)?   YES/NO

6 Conditions (see note 6)
Do you consent to the plans being passed subject to conditions where appropriate?   YES/NO

7 Fees (see notes 3, 4 and separate Guidance Note on Fees for information)
1 If Schedule 1 work please state number of dwellings:
2 If Schedule 2 work please state floor area: m²
3 If Schedule 3 work please state the estimated cost of work excluding VAT: £
Plan fee: £   plus VAT: £   Total: £

8 Completion certificate
Do you require a completion certificate following satisfactory completion of the building work?   YES/NO

9 Additional information
Do you agree to the determination period being extended from five weeks to two months?   YES/NO
Type of Heating to be installed:
Type of Drainage: Foul   Surface Water

10 Statement
This notice is given in relation to the building work as described, and is submitted in accordance with
Regulation 11(1)(b) and is accompanied by the appropriate fee. I understand that further fees will be
payable following the first inspection by the local authority.

Name: Signature: Date:

Figure 12. Detail from full set of plans

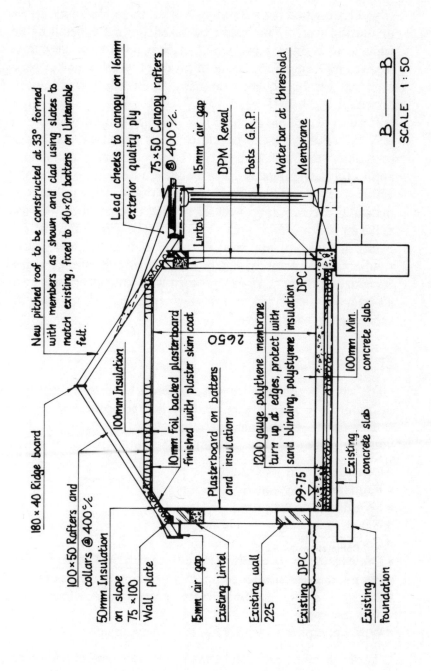

New pitched roof to be constructed at 33° formed with members as shown and clad using slates to match existing, fixed to 40×20 battens on Untearable felt.

180 × 40 Ridge board

Lead cheeks to canopy on 16mm exterior quality ply

75×50 Canopy rafters @ 400%.

15mm air gap

DPM Reveal

Posts G.R.P.

Waterbar at threshold

Membrane

100mm Insulation

10mm Foil backed plasterboard finished with plaster skim coat

Plasterboard on battens and insulation

1200 gauge polythene membrane turn up at edges, protect with sand blinding, polystyrene insulation

DPC

100mm Min. concrete slab.

Existing concrete slab

2650

99·75

100×50 Rafters and collars @ 400%.

50mm Insulation on slope 75 ×100

Wall plate

15mm air gap

Existing Lintel

Existing wall 225

Existing DPC

Existing foundation

Lintol

B — B

SCALE 1 : 50

87

Approval of applications

If you have opted for a Building Notice, there obviously isn't any delay in starting work. You might be asked for more detail or be advised while work is in progress that changes have to be made, but you won't receive any formal advance notification of whether or not your application has been approved. You just give the appropriate notice and get on with it.

If you are submitting a Full Plans Application, the local authority may take five weeks to decide on your proposal, and possibly eight (but only with your agreement). However, unlike Planning Approval applications, the onus is upon the local authority to come back to you within the stated time limit. If they don't, the application is automatically deemed approved! They might come back and ask you to make amendements or provide more details. When the plans have been passed a notice of approval is issued. If it is refused, you can either resubmit your plans with amendments or, ultimately, appeal to the Secretary of State. You can proceed with your proposed work at only 48 hours' notice – but at your own risk, in that the work might not subsequently be approved.

Site inspections

Once work begins you (or your builder) have to inform the building inspector at certain stages so that he can examine the work being carried out. There are nine statutory stages, depending on the extent of your renovation, and each requires a minimum period of notice:

- Commencement – 48 hours
- Foundations excavated – 24 hours
- Foundations constructed – 24 hours
- Damp-proof course – 24 hours
- Concrete oversite – 24 hours
- Drains and sewers before being covered up – 24 hours
- Drains and sewers after completion – within five days of completion
- Occupation of a building before completion – within 5 days before part occupied
- Works completed – within five days of completion

Other inspections can also be made, i.e. on concrete reinforcement, fire precaution work and any other work which may be hidden once the works have been completed. Be careful that your builder complies, otherwise *you* may have to pay for the extra time it takes him to dig down and expose a covered foundation.

You must send in a commencement and a completion notice (see Figure 13). All other notifications may be given by 'phone. In return most local authorities will attempt to make site inspections within 24 hours of request and often will call the same day if given notice early in the morning. Don't be surprised if you meet several different people – building supervision involves fire prevention officers and environmental health inspectors as well as the building control officer. Remember that officers are out on site much of the time, so it is better to make appointments either early in the morning or after they have returned later in the day.

Fees

There are fees to be paid for these inspections and they are your responsibility, not the builder's. Your building regulations department will provide a list of current charges. Building Notice fees only become payable after the first site inspection following commencement of work. With Full Plans part of the total fees have to accompany your application for it to be allowed to proceed at all.

Certificate of Completion

When work has finished a final inspection takes place and, providing the completed works comply with regulations, you will be issued with a Certificate of Completion, which might be charged for. You should indicate that you will want this document when you first submit your plans. It can come in very useful, especially if you want to sell the property and demonstrate that the building work has been passed and accepted by the local authority.

Approved inspectors

A word about approved inspectors. At the time of writing, only the local authority are empowered to administer the building regulations. However, the government intend to introduce competition by allowing private building inspectors, known as Approved Inspectors, to carry out pretty much the same functions as the council's Building Control.

Figure 13.

Westminster District Surveyors' Service

To the District Surveyor   Reg. No: ....

BUILDING REGULATIONS: NOTICE OF COMMENCEMENT

Address of Premises: ....

Work:...

I hereby give 48 hours notice in accordance with Regulation 14 that the above work will

start on: ....

Signature: ....Name in Capitals:...................................

Company:...

Address: ....

Telephone: .... Date: ....

Statutory Notifications under Regulation 14 (**except** for commencement and
completion) may be made to the District Surveyor by telephone for this work.

City of Westminster   PLANNING AND TRANSPORTATION DEPARTMENT (01/93) S/BC.38

Westminster District Surveyors' Service

To the District Surveyor   Reg. No:...................................

BUILDING REGULATIONS: NOTICE OF COMPLETION

Address of Premises: ....

Work: ....

I hereby give 7 days notice in accordance with Regulation14 that the above
works will be complete on: ....

Signature: ....   Name in Capitals: ....

Date: ....

City of Westminster   PLANNING AND TRANSPORTATION DEPARTMENT (01/93) S/BC.39

If you are approached, or indeed prefer to use the services of an Approved Inspector, make sure that they are registered with the Construction Industry Council. You are also perfectly entitled to ask for references, just to make sure that they are suitable. Lastly, you might find that when using an Approved Inspector the building regulations application procedure and the details required differ slightly from those requested by the council.

What happens if you go ahead without approval

Depending upon how naughty you have been and how greatly you have irritated the Building Regs people, they can penalise you in either or both of the following ways:

- By serving a Notice under Sec 36B of the Building Act 1984, which orders you (i.e. the owner) to take down the offending structure or bring it into compliance with the regulations, usually within 28 days.

- By prosecuting you under Sec 35B of the Building Act 1984. There are standard fines, amended each year, but they go up to £5000 plus £50 for each day that the regulations remain breached. If you have a builder doing the work on your behalf they may well try to prosecute him (although he will say that he is simply acting on your instructions) and then in addition, serve the Sec 36 Notice on you as the owner. Furthermore, the local authority have the power to put the work right themselves and charge you for it.

Of course, there is always a temptation to just do the work without permission and hope that you will get away with it, especially if it is mainly internal and less likely to be noticed by neighbours, etc. And it has to be said that if the work is subsequently found to be up to standard, you could get away with just a slapped wrist and retrospective approval. However, bear in mind that if you are in breach of requirements, the Building Regs people can serve a Notice on you for anything up to a year after the work has been done, and prosecute you for a maximum of six months after the event. The only loophole here is that it is often difficult to prove exactly when work was done (unless there are third party witnesses) and the offender can just swear blind that the work took place outside those time limits and is therefore exempt from intervention. On the other hand, as and when you try to sell, the purchaser's solicitors will want confirmation that building regs approval has been obtained and the building is up to scratch. Ultimately, the decision has to be yours, but I don't think it's worth risking the safety and saleability of your property just to avoid a little extra work.

Summary

Building regs can be quite complicated, but by following the proper procedure there is no reason why you shouldn't manage the application yourself. In summary, it is as follows:

- Prepare sketch plans if necessary for preliminary discussions with Building Control Officer (which will probably entail professional help)
- Prepare detailed plans, calculations, specifications, etc. (again, probably with the help of a professional)
- Consider if completion certificate will be given, or should be applied for
- Send to building control office full plans (FP) or building notice (BN)
- Pay fee with application (FP only)
- Await notification
  - acknowledgement
  - request for more information
  - request for extensions of time
- Decision
  - within five weeks or, by agreement, two months from date submitted
  - rejection (may be passed if you subsequently amend plans to comply)
  - plans passed
- Give notice of intended commencement
  - start work
  - continue work and comply with building regulations
  - give progress notices
  - receive inspection visits from Building Control Officers
  - pay inspection fee (FP) or building notice fee (BN)
- Give notice of completion
- Receive completion of certificate if applicable.

Now that didn't hurt, did it?!

UTILITIES

Now is also a good time to organise your utilities, principally to make sure that wherever appropriate they are connected and ready for when the builder starts work.

Electricity

Supply: if you have just bought your property the first job will be to contact your local electricity company and ask to be connected. There are twelve electricity companies in England and Wales and two in Scotland, and each has its own application form, but you will be asked for much the same information:

- your address;
- the day you want the supply to commence;
- the maximum power required (they can calculate this by asking you to tick boxes describing what you will be using the electricity for);
- the period for which you want the electricity (e.g. six months, or indefinitely).

Having received this information, the electricity company is then obliged by law to give you a supply. There is no charge for taking over an account. If, however, your property doesn't already have electricity, the supplier has to lay down lines for this purpose. There is a charge for this and it will vary according to the length of cable needed to connect your property to the mains.

Rewiring: once inside your house the electrical fittings and wiring are completely your own responsibility. The rather curious thing about electricity is that there is still nothing in law which states that you have to conform to any set procedure when working with electrics. While in Scotland the building regulations make provision for standards of electrical work, the rest of the UK is still only considering legislation. It is therefore vital that you (or your builder) employ only qualified people to do the work, preferably a member of the NICEIC (National Inspection Council for Electrical Installation Contracting) or the ECA (Electrical Contractors' Association). In any case, a reputable contractor will follow the Best Practice Standards issued by the Institute of Electrical Engineers, and issue a certificate stating that his work conforms to these recommendations (see Figure 14). This certificate

Figure 14.

Form WR1

COMPLETION AND INSPECTION CERTIFICATE

(as prescribed in British Standard 7671: 1992 the IEE Wiring Regulations Sixteenth Edition)

DETAILS OF THE INSTALLATION New ☐ Alteration*☐ Addition*☐*to existing*

Client:..

Address:..

Description of Installation...

DESIGN

I/We being the person(s) responsible (as indicated by my/our signatures below) for the Design of the electrical installation, particulars of which are described on Page 2 of this form CERTIFY that the said work for which I/we have been responsible is to the best of my/our knowledge and belief in accordance with the Regulations for Electrical Installations published by the Institution of Electrical Engineers, 16th Edition, amended to (note 3.) (date ....) except for the departures, if any, stated in this Certificate.

The extent of liability of the signatory is limited to the work described above as the subject of this Certificate.

For the DESIGN of the installation:

Name (In Block Letters):

Position:

For and on behalf of:

Address:

(note 2.) Signature   (note 3.) Date:

CONSTRUCTION

I/We being the person(s) responsible (as indicated by my/our signatures below) for the Construction of the electrical installation, particulars of which are described on Page 2 of this form CERTIFY that the said work for which I/we have been responsible is to the best of my/our knowledge and belief in accordance with the Regulations for Electrical Installations published by the Institution of Electrical Engineers, 16th Edition, amended to (note 3.) (date ....) except for the departures, if any, stated in this Certificate.

The extent of liability of the signatory is limited to the work described above as the subject of this Certificate.

For the CONSTRUCTION of the installation:

Name (In Block Letters):

Position:

For an on behalf of:

Address:

(note 2.) Signature: (note 3.) Date:

INSPECTION AND TEST

I/We being the person(s) responsible (as indicated by my/our signatures below) for the Inspection and Test of the electrical installation, particulars of which are described on Page 3 of this form, CERTIFY that the said work for which I/we have been responsible is to the best of my/our knowledge and belief in accordance with the Regulations for Electrical Installations published by the Institute of Electrical Engineers, 16th Edition, amended on (note 3.) (date ....) except for departures, if any, stated in this Certificate.

Departures from Regulations | YES   NO | other than by Reg 120–4 or 120–5.

The extent of liability of the signatory is limited to the work described above as the subject of this Certificate.

For the INSPECTION AND TEST of the installation:

Name (In Block Letters):

Position:

For and on behalf of:

Address:

I RECOMMEND that this installation be further inspected and tested after an interval of not more than ..... years. (5.)
(note 2.) Signature: (note 3.) Date:
          See notes overleaf   page 1 of 5 pages

This form is protected by copyright. Reproduced by courtesy of the Institute of Electrical Engineers from its Guidance Note 3, Inspection and testing.

may be required by your local electricity company, who have the right to disconnect your supply if they are dissatisfied with the standard of work or if it fails their tests. If you are applying for a mortgage to buy the property, the mortgage company may insist upon an electrical survey as a precondition of the loan.

Gas

Supply: British Gas is the only mains supplier of gas in the UK. At the time of writing it is divided into twelve regional gas companies, which by 1995 will become five 'business units', each organised by function (e.g. installation and servicing) rather than by region. If you are moving into a property and simply want to take over the account, a 'phone call to your local gas office will suffice. If your property doesn't have a gas supply and as part of the renovation you want one, the gas company will have to come and install a connection from the mains pipe to your house and also a meter (either internal or external according to your preference). The charge for this will depend entirely on where your property is situated in relation to the local gas main, and can vary from virtually nothing to thousands of pounds (which will make it impractical in some cases). The time it takes will also depend upon the complexity of the job. Given that this could cause significant delay to any renovation, you should arrange for an appointment well before any works are due to begin.

Gas appliances: while British Gas holds responsibility for the gas main and gas meter, all pipework within your property from the outlet of the gas meter is your responsibility alone. What's more, it is now illegal to work on any gas pipe without being Corgi registered; so, if you are using a builder, kitchen fitter or plumber, make sure that they are. Obviously, British Gas is one of the largest contractors in the business and can do the work, but your local gas showroom will also cary a list of 'non British Gas' Corgi registered installers. Just in case you need persuading, a badly fitted gas appliance can leak carbon monoxide, and poison you.

Telephone

Connection: if you simply want to keep the existing telephone line and have it connected in your name, all you have to do is ring BT on 150 (or Mercury, as the case may be) and make that request. BT make a reconnection charge of £21.28 + VAT (1994 rate) and all new customers are subject to a credit check. The charge for installing a new telephone is £99 + VAT. Remember that even if you want to use your own 'phone, BT will charge you for 'rental' of the existing line.

New lines: if, however, you plan to gut the property, you should dial the operator and ask for Freephone 'Dial Before You Dig'. The engineer will advise you and if necessary, come and investigate the site to show you where existing cables lie or where new ones should be laid. If you live in a remote area with no telephone system at all, BT will supply the service in the cheapest and most practical way possible; this normally means installing a telegraph pole, at a cost of £99 – 150. If however, you want an underground cable, the bill can run into the hundreds as it is charged on a time-related basis. Alternatively, BT will supply the duct and cable free of charge (amazing but true) if your builder is able and willing to do the job, and then just check it over to make sure the cable has been laid properly.

Water

Supply: there are ten big water and sewerage companies in the UK and a number of smaller 'water only' supply companies. Whether you are new to the property and simply want to take over the supply, or you need to have a new supply laid on, you should call your local water company for advice and quotations. The cost of connecting a new water and sewerage supply will vary depending on the length of pipe that needs to be laid from the water main to the property. But there is also an 'infrastructure' charge, i.e. the cost of providing the extra capacity in the system; in London, for example, this is £410 + VAT for water and £336 + VAT for sewerage – charges vary from region to region.

Installations: whether you are having new or replacement plumbing work in your property, it is a legal requirement that it complies with the Water Bylaws; these exist primarily to prevent contamination and wastage of your water supply and to protect your health. For instance, you are obliged to inform your local water authority if you plan to install a bidet, new loo, fit a garden tap or connect anything to the rising main pipe. Changes to the soil/waste side are currently covered by Building Regulations. These bylaws do vary slightly from region to region, so you should always contact your local water company for an up to date Bylaws Guide

Are you still awake? Sorry, but as I said, no apologies for the length of this chapter; it simply goes to prove that if you want to do any job properly, it's the preparation that counts!

APPROVALS CHECKLIST

Type of work	Planning permission	Building regs approval
Repair or decoration, inside or out	No	No
Replacing windows or doors	Only if they project beyond the front wall facing a highway	No, provided window opening is not enlarged or the window is not of structural importance
Electrical work	No	No, but must comply with IEE regulations
Plumbing	No	Yes, if it affects soil/waste. Not for simple replacement, but check with water company for new installations
Installing central heating	No	Yes, but not for simple replacement
Installing satellite dish	No, if it does not extend above roof level and is less than 70cm diameter	No
Internal structural alterations	No	Yes
Loft conversion	No, provided volume of house is unchanged and highest part of roof not raised. But yes, possibly, if you add a loft window	Yes
Building garden wall or fence	Yes, if more than 1 metre high next to a road or more than 2m high elsewhere	No (unless it is a retaining wall)
Laying path or driveway	No, but must have highways dept's approval if new and crosses a pavement or verge	No

APPROVALS CHECKLIST (continued)

Type of work	Planning permission	Building regs approval
Installing a swimming pool	Possibly, depends on size	Yes, indoors, possibly outdoors
Building a porch	Not if within 'permitted allowance'	No
Building an extension or conservatory	Not if within 'permitted allowance', except in conservation area	Yes, possibly
Building a garage	Yes, in conservation area if within 5m of house must be within 'permitted allowance' otherwise check	Possibly
Demolition	No, unless in conservation area. Yes, if proposing to rebuild	No, for complete detached house; yes for partial, semi-detached or terrace
Converting house into flats	Yes	Yes
Converting house to business premises	Yes	Yes

Note: When dealing with **listed buildings** or buildings in conservation areas, advice should be sought from the planning and building regulations department for *any* alterations internal or external.
(Table reproduced by kind permission of the NHIC.)

CHAPTER FIVE

Understanding the Renovation Process

As you have no doubt heard many times, the purchase of your home is probably the biggest financial commitment you are ever likely to make. Why is it then that people are so cavalier about protecting that investment? They spend weeks or months searching for the best mortgage deal, saving a few pounds wherever possible. Yet when it comes to the refurbishment of their home, they happily engage a builder without any real understanding of the work that is about to take place. There is no reason why you shouldn't organise the builder yourself and save a lot of money in professional management fees. But to do so effectively you need some basic technical understanding of the various structural elements within your property and the order in which that work is usually carried out. Ideally you should acquire this knowledge before dealing with any builders, so that you can identify when things are not going according to plan and stay in control of the operation rather than be at the mercy of the builder's reports. If the builder realises that you are clued up as to what he should and shouldn't be doing, he is much less likely to try to pull a fast one! So, to begin at the beginning . . .

THE STRUCTURAL ELEMENTS OF A HOUSE

It is of course impossible to give one all-encompassing description of the structural elements of a house - they vary greatly, depending upon whether you live in an old country cottage or a twentieth-century town house. Moreover, it wasn't until the 1930s' National Building Regulations that standards and methods of construction were brought into line throughout the country and previous to that it was very much a case of local variations on a theme. So to simplify matters I have used the example of a more modern house to illustrate the basic elements (see Figure 15; the numbers in the text refer to those in the Figure), but have highlighted in the text any significant differences with older buildings. What I am really trying to give you is a basic appreciation of what makes up a house, so that you can at least follow the builder when he starts rambling on about purlins, floor decks and inner skins. I realise that I am on dangerous ground here, as people in the building trade advise me that giving the client 'a little bit of knowledge' is a bad thing (i.e. they interfere) – but I can't help feeling that, far from being threatened, any decent builder would welcome some intelligent understanding on the part of the client. So here goes . . .

Groundworks

These basically comprise everything up to damp-proof course and include:

Footings

Modern houses are built on foundations called footings; these are basically trenches filled with concrete to 15 cm (6 inches) below ground level (called trench fill footings) or trenches part filled to a minimum depth of 60 cm (23½ inches) below ground level (called strip footings – 1), on which the first sections of supporting wall are built up to damp-proof course level. Their function is to take the loadbearing part of the house below ground to where the ground is firm and protected from the effects of frost, drying out and shrinkage. As a result of that requirement, the depth of the footings varies depending upon ground conditions, but is not usually less than 750 mm (29½ inches). Those of you living in houses built on clay are likely to have deeper footings, primarily to protect the structure from the effects of clay drying out and causing movement. Those of you who were living in clay-based south-east England during the drought of 1976 will probably not want reminding! (see Figure 16).

If you live in a house of some age – 100 years old or more – don't be surprised to find that there are no foundations to speak of. Larger properties may well have them, but humbler constructions, often stone cottages, can have very shallow footings or walls which start only just below ground level. Scary but true! Ground conditions also play their

101

Figure 15.

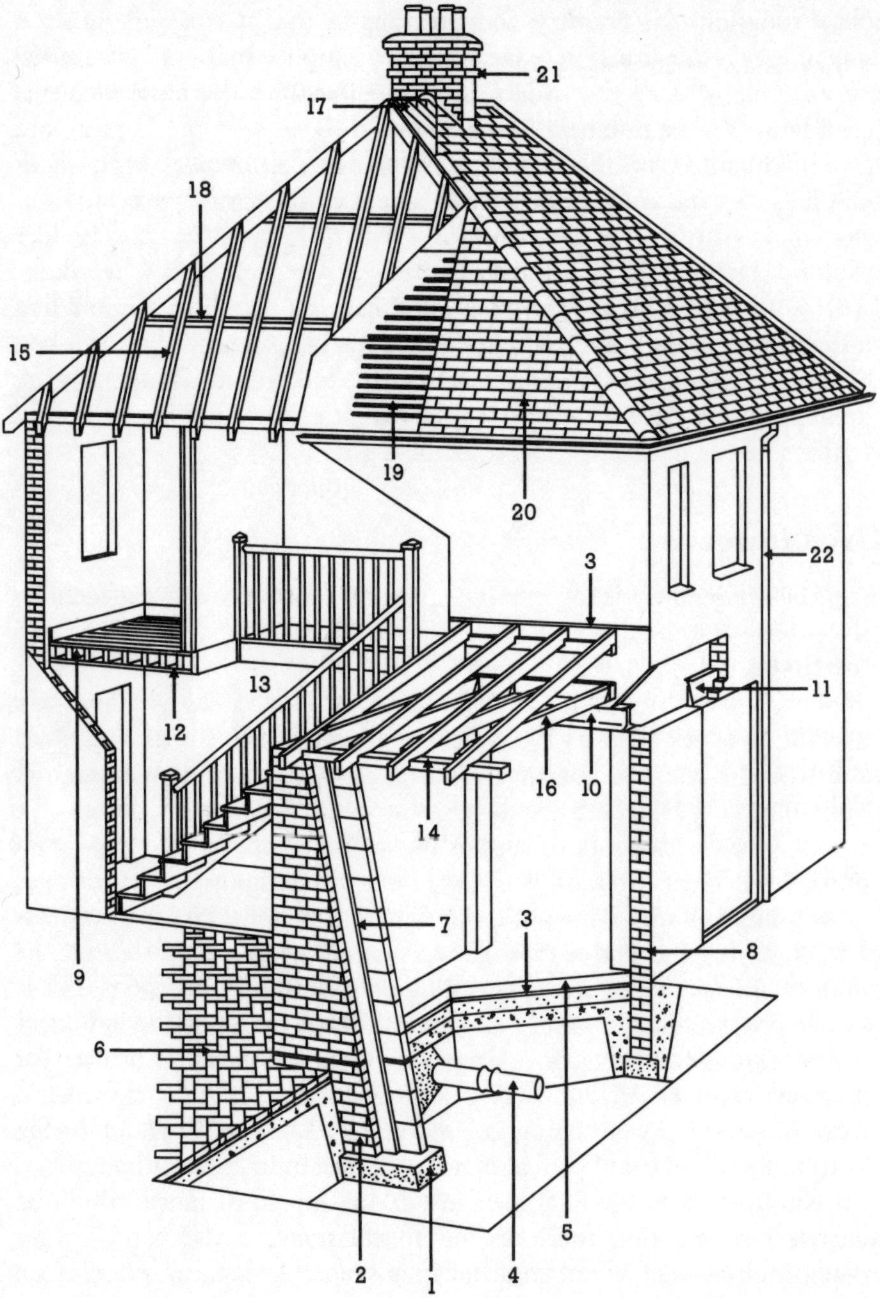

Figure 16. Strip Footing

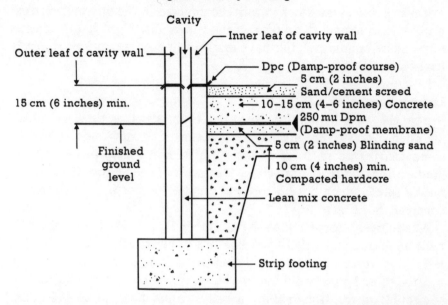

part: old houses built on rock are less likely to have foundations than those built on clay, because they would not have been deemed necessary. The plus side is that older houses often have thicker, slightly damper and more flexible walls which are better at accommodating ground movement. The Society for the Protection of Ancient Buildings (SPAB) can provide lots of information on the construction of old buildings, especially those built before 1850.

Walls up to damp-proof course (2)

The supporting walls of the house, external and possibly internal, extend from the footings. Since the 1930s and to achieve better insulation, many external walls have been built as a cavity wall construction, i.e. comprising both an inner and outer layer (skin) with a small cavity in between, the purpose of which is to prevent moisture penetrating both the inner and outer wall. These external walls are then built up from the footings to the damp-proof course (dpc) level, which is itself normally a minimum of 150 mm (6 inches) above the finished ground level outside. For those of you not in the know, a dpc is a physical barrier inserted into buildings to prevent moisture from the ground rising and causing damp in the living space. A dpc can be made of bitumised felt, plastic (sometimes blue bricks, slate or stone in houses built before the turn of the century) or be chemically injected. It is used in various other places around the house, e.g. where the roof abuts the brickwork, but is most commonly encountered in the internal/external walls of a building at or near ground level (3). Until late Victorian times many buildings didn't have dpc, but of course may subsequently have had it fitted.

Inner floor slabs (5)

Within the walls lie the floor surfaces. Floor slabs, as they are called, are often concrete. The normal construction is 10 cm (4 inches) of well-compacted hardcore, 5 cm (2 inches) of blinding sand (normally low grade beach sand) to protect the damp-proof membrane (basically a plastic sheet) which lies on top and finally, 10–15 cm (4–6 inches) of concrete. (See Figure 16.)

Alternatively, some houses have timber floors, which are basically built upon and supported by sleeper walls, constructed below the dpc level. You won't normally find timber floors in a pre-dpc house, simply because those houses would not be damp free and any timber would be susceptible to rot, thus making it rather impractical. In an old house you might find anything from beaten earth floors to stone flags, almost always without a damp-proof membrane.

Generally speaking, builders carrying out renovation work aren't terrible keen on groundworks, mainly because the problems which arise are usually unforeseen and therefore rather troublesome. Older properties can be particularly awkward because of the variations in building practice and standards. If you are the owner of an ancient pile, try doing a bit of research into the property to find out when, how and upon what it was built. Also consider asking representatives of the appropriate utilities to look over their records for the property, and to come along and advise you as to where their pipes, cables, etc. might be. It should be a free service and can save a lot of hassle later on.

The oversite

The oversite is the term used to describe the ground outside the building and includes what is to become garden, driveway, patios etc.

The structure above dpc level

This comprises walls (including windows, doors and upstairs floors), services, ceilings, stairwells, roof, chimneys and external pipes.

Walls

If you have cavity walls (7) the external wall (outer skin) will probably be built of brick or concrete block, the latter of which is then rendered. The inner wall can be brick (often found in houses of the 1940s and 1950s) or concrete block, normally concrete because it is cheaper. More recently, Themalite insulating blocks will have been used. Older houses may have solid brick walls (8) or solid stone (often found in cottages). I should also mention timber-frame houses, which are basically houses where the inner skin of the cavity wall is constructed of timber stud work, which in turn supports all floor and roof loads. Since it has only become popular within the last 10/15 years in Britain you are unlikely to have a timber-frame house which needs renovating. But, if you have to demolish walls because of inadequate footings, you could consider a timber-frame replacement as its construction is such that it doesn't require footings to be as substantial as a concrete block wall. If you do have a timber-frame house and want to have work done to it, get a copy of 'Living in a Timber and Brick Home' (from the Timber and Brick Homes Information Council) for specialist advice on what should and shouldn't be done to the cavity walls.

In a property of more than one storey you have what is called a 'floor deck' (9) at first floor level; a floor deck is really just another term for a floor and regardless of the age of the house this is nearly always timber, i.e. joists covered in chipboard or floorboards. The walls then extend up to roof level. Windows and doors are installed either as the wall is built or the appropriate openings are left in the brickwork and the windows/doors added later.

You will find that external walls are nearly always built of the same materials at both ground and first floor level, i.e. they are always masonry. But internally there is often a distinction; downstairs internal partition walls are often of a single skin block, because they need to be loadbearing and carry the floor joists for the first floor. However, when you get to the first floor, the roof may be of such a construction that it carries the roof load to the external walls without the need for any supporting wall inside the building, and so the upstairs internal walls can be made from timber studwork which has the benefit of being cheap and lightweight. Timber studwork is basically a row of timbers 100×50 mm or 75×50 mm (4×2 inches or 3×2 inches) arranged in a row and clad each side in plasterboard, the whole of which forms a partition. This means that the upstairs floorplan need not match the one downstairs, giving greater flexibility to planning and layout.

Generally speaking then, if a downstairs wall is built of block, brick or stone (i.e. masonry) and corresponds to a masonry wall above, then that downstairs wall is likely to be loadbearing. But be careful – even if it doesn't correspond to a wall above it might be supporting a floor load; to find out take a look at the floor boards. They should run perpendicular to any floor joists which bear on a wall (i.e. if the floor boards run north/south, the floor joists will almost certainly run east/west). Exceptions to the rule are chipboard, which can run in the same direction as the floor joists. Of course, not all ground floor walls are loadbearing. Just ask yourself if there is anything sitting on that wall or supported by it which would fall down if that wall were taken away and, without wishing to be too flippant, that is your answer! Again, in old properties, internal walls might be built from very different materials – stone if they were loadbearing or lathe and plaster on studwork if they were not. Lathes, by the way, are simply strips of sweet chestnut nailed close together on the studs and plastered to give a solid finish. Even today, in such places as the Forest of Dean, you can find groves of sweet chestnut originally grown for just that purpose. Lathe and plaster is also found in ceilings – very messy, dusty stuff to remove, so be warned. Nailing plasterboard on top of lathe and plaster can save this trouble.

One last word about walls. If a loadbearing wall has been knocked through, e.g. to open up a room, you should find a steel or concrete lintel inserted above the opening to hold up the structure in place of the supporting wall which has been removed. The steel version is the famous RSJ (10) – rolled steel joist or catnic lintel (11). If there isn't one, do something about it quickly!

Services (4)

Leading into the house you may have pipes for oil, gas or water and cables for electricity or telephone. Leading out of the house you have foul drains. Each different utility has to lie a different depth below ground level: water pipes between 750 mm and 1200 mm ($29\frac{1}{2}$ and $47\frac{1}{4}$ inches), gas pipes 450 mm – 600 mm ($17\frac{3}{4}$ – $23\frac{1}{2}$ inches), telephone lines 300 mm – 400 mm ($11\frac{3}{4}$ – $15\frac{3}{4}$ inches) and electricity cables 300 mm – 450 mm ($11\frac{3}{4}$ – $47\frac{1}{4}$ inches). Having entered the house, the pipes and cables are normally concealed by the internal walls and floors, although there may be visible elements such as extractor fans. Older systems may not be so well disguised and you may have unsightly pipes or cables running along the internal walls. In a totally unmodernised house more than 50 years old, you probably won't find any central heating or electricity. What's more, it is invariably expensive and quite awkward to put in, largely because of the difficulty of putting pipes and cables through what are often solid stone walls.

Leaving the house are the foul drains, in which foul water from WCs, sinks, wash hand basins and washing machines is collected and passed to the main foul sewer, which is outside your property. In rural areas a foul sewer may not exist and a septic tank will be used instead. This is distinct from the storm water system which collects surface water from drives and paths and rainwater from roofs via guttering and downpipes – and you need special permission to direct storm water into the foul drain system. In towns, storm water is usually removed from the property in a special storm sewer. In rural areas, storm water is directed to a soakaway.

Ceilings (12)
These are normally simple plasterboard or in older properties, lathe and plaster.

Stairwell (13)
The hole for the stairwell is normally made when the first-floor floor joists are put in. The actual staircase is fitted last, mainly to save it from damage caused by the hooves of stampeding builders.

Roof
The roof is normally constructed on top of what is called the wallplate (piece of timber running around the top of the wall – 14). If the wall is built of concrete block or brick the wallplate is normally bedded in mortar on the inner skin (leaf) of the wall and held down by metal straps. On top of that goes the roof structure. In a modern construction you will probably have what is called a trussed roof, i.e. a series of large factory-made triangular shaped wooden fabrications, strengthened with diagonal braces, usually set 600 mm (23½ inches) apart, then felted, battened and tiled (see Figure 17). The more traditional pitched roof construction is called a cut roof and is made from individual pieces of timber laid in situ to form rafters (15), ceiling joists (16) and a ridge (17), which are held together by the strengthening power of purlins (18) and binders. Older properties used boarding (like floorboards) before battens (19) came into existence and then slates, thatch

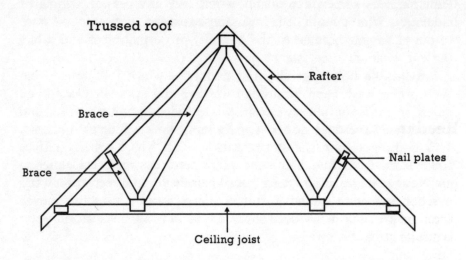

Figure 17.

Trussed roof

Rafter

Brace

Nail plates

Brace

Ceiling joist

or perhaps fire clay tiles (20) for the final finish. The choice of roofing material (and for that matter, walls) often depended on the natural resources of the locality and what was least expensive to acquire.

Note: Flat roofs merit a special mention as they are of a completely different construction and although not very durable or desirable, are nonetheless quite common. Basically, they are constructed of joists covered with a 'firing' strip (a tapering piece of wood which gives the roof a very slight pitch of 50 mm/2 inches or so, necessary to make sure that water etc. will be able to run off the surface), which is in turn covered with plywood and then three layers of felt interspersed with bitumen. Generally speaking, flat roofs do not last more than about 15 years and need much more maintenance than a pitched roof, usually because their flat surface means that anything falling onto them i.e. snow, rain, leaves, etc., does more damage than it would to a pitched roof. Try to avoid them if at all possible.

Chimneys (21)

These are not just built on to the top of the house (and therefore not supported by the roof) but run right through it from the foundations upwards. Chimneys are a very important part of the structure of a house and should be carefully maintained and inspected for damage to brickwork etc., particularly to prevent a fire hazard.

External pipes (22)
Guttering, downpipes, etc. direct water and waste away from the building so that it doesn't collect and cause damage.

HEATING AND ELECTRICAL SYSTEMS

Heating systems

You may have an antiquated system that needs updating, or like us in our Welsh cottage, no system at all. Whichever, your very best course of action is to seek the advice of a qualified heating engineer (either direct or through your builder), who will be able to gauge your particular requirements. But before you do, here is a basic rundown of the systems you are most likely to have and the other options available:

Fuel types
Depending on where you live and available services, you have a choice of natural gas, LPG (Liquefied Petroleum Gas or Calor), oil, coal, wood or electricity. Remember that the Clean Air Act of 1993 prohibits the use of wood or coal throughout most of London and also in other large conurbations. Looking purely at running costs, coal and oil are approximately 20 per cent more expensive than natural gas, LPG 3 times the cost and electricity a hefty 3.8 – 4 times as much. Gas also has the advantage of being convenient, quick, cheap and controllable. So is oil, but you do have to have the tank topped up and it can be a bit smelly. Coal and wood are fine but rather labour intensive and dirty and electricity (via a storage radiator system) is often criticised for not providing people with heat when they actually need it most, i.e. in the evening. Unsurprisingly then, the majority of houses are supplied by gas, or oil when gas is unavailable.

Systems
1. The traditional type of heating system is water-based, sometimes referred to as a 'wet' system (see Figure 18). Water is heated in a boiler and distributed round the house via pipes to radiators; the radiators get hot and the room gets warm. The water (called primary water) used for heating the radiators is unsuitable for domestic use, so a secondary system operates at the same time whereby the water

Figure 18. A Wet System

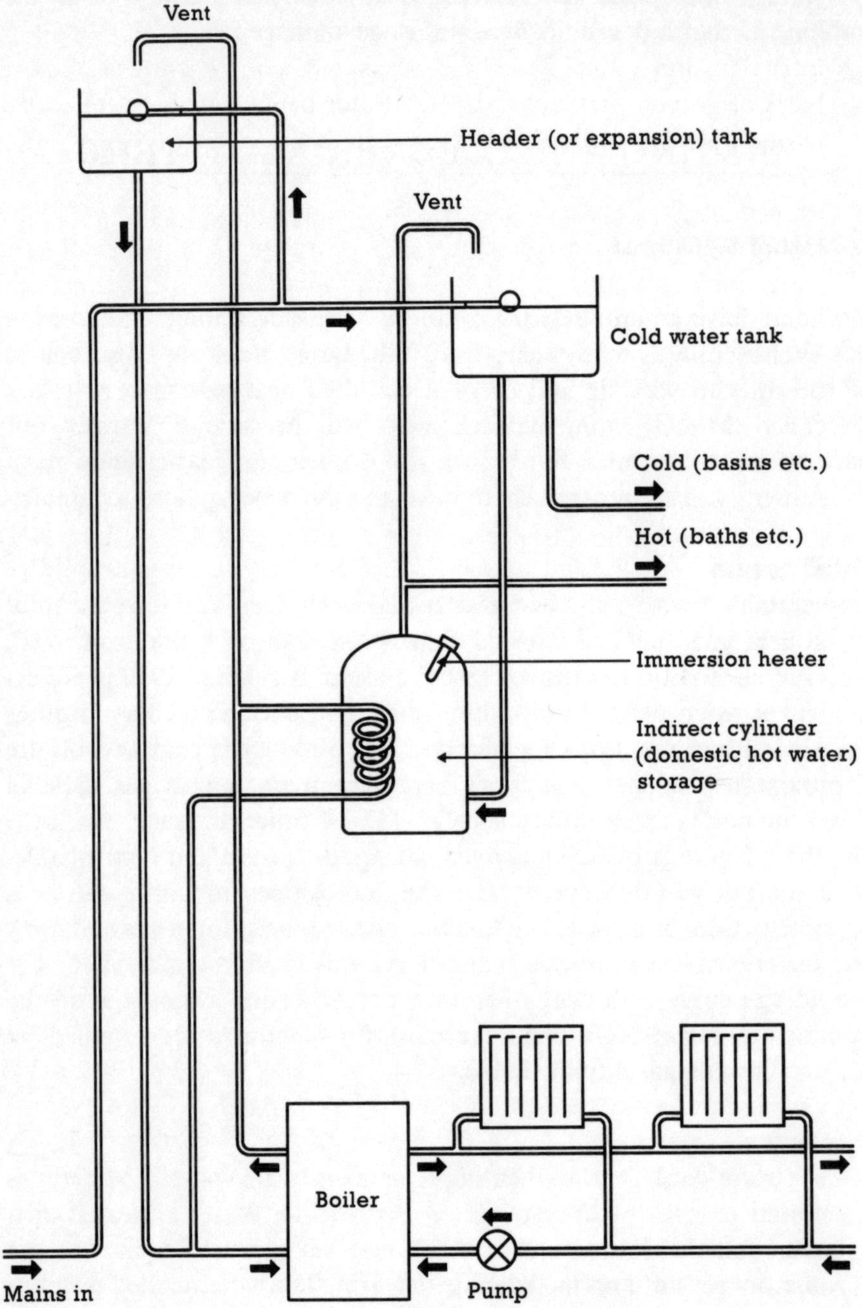

Vent

Header (or expansion) tank

Vent

Cold water tank

Cold (basins etc.)

Hot (baths etc.)

Immersion heater

Indirect cylinder
(domestic hot water)
storage

Boiler

Mains in

Pump

from the boiler is also passed through a coil which sits inside a hot water cylinder and heats the clean water in the cylinder, which itself has come from a cold water storage tank (normally found in the loft). This hot water is used for baths, etc. The system works on the basis of gravity pressure – the hot water being forced out of the top of the cylinder as the cold water enters the bottom. This happens every time a hot tap is turned on. Keeping the primary system topped up is a second, smaller, header (or expansion) tank, filled from the mains. Domestic cold water is drawn directly from the cold water tank, which is in turn fed from the mains and supplies wash hand basins and lavatory cisterns. Drinking water, e.g. from the kitchen sink, is fed directly from the mains. This type of system can be run on gas, oil, coal or even wood (if you own a forest) and is called 'central heating' because the heat comes from a central source.

If you have this type of system and it is in good working order but rather old, it may be possible to simply replace the radiators and boiler and keep the pipes. If, however, the pipes are very old, made of lead or steel or full of scale, it is probably worth starting from scratch. Equally, if you want to add more rads (radiators) to the system you may need to get a bigger boiler and in turn, larger pipes. On the question of how big the radiators should be, this is really where the expert knowledge of a heating engineer comes into play. He will use a number of factors such as room size, window glazing, and roof and wall insulation, to estimate the heat loss from each room and thus quantify the level of heat needed to keep it warm.

If you are going to change the system it might be worth considering the more modern combination boiler, which operates on a sealed system and produces both domestic hot water and heating water. The installation costs are low – there is no expansion tank in the loft, no hot water cylinder and less pipework – but the boiler itself is more expensive to buy and maintain and there are more things that can go wrong with it. A combination boiler can be fitted in any house that has a gas supply and must be near an exterior wall for ventilation purposes.

I have concentrated on central heating because it is now the most common form of heating. But you may have other systems which, although they are not true 'central heating', are perfectly adequate and do not need replacing: gas fires, for example, only heat the room they are in but for anyone who doesn't want full central heating they are a good cheap alternative. So are open coal fires, wood fires or wood burning stoves, although they are rather more labour intensive and can get messy (you may be denied this option by living in a smoke-free zone). Any of the above options may be fitted with a back boiler which will provide some heat for a hot water cylinder and/or radiators. But do bear in mind that the heat output of back boilers is generally low and if your house is anything other than small, the results will be disappointing. And in case you have any romantic notions about woodburning stoves (as I did), just remember that the heat from only one ton of coal is equivalent to four tonnes of wood – so as I said, unless you own a forest . . .

2. 'Dry' heating systems include electric night storage heaters, which are cheap to buy and quick to fit. They do however, have the failing of delivering most heat in the morning when you are probably going to work and least need it. Remember also, that you cannot use the existing ring main or fuse board for them – you need a separate fuse board and an off-peak meter. The other type of dry heating is the blown air system, whereby air is blown through a gas or oil fired heater and then passes around the house through conduits in cavity floors and is blown through wall vents. This is not really practical for anywhere other than new houses because of the difficulty of inserting floor ducts.

Electrical systems

Depending on the age of your property, there could be a significant difference in the way it is wired. Older, unmodernised properties will probably have 'radial' wiring, a system whereby each power socket has its own wire connecting it to its own fuse on the fuseboard. There is no fuse in the plug, which is of the 15 amp, round-pin variety. And there are separate fuseboards for power sockets, lights and large appliances such as cookers. As you can imagine, the result is something like Spaghetti Junction with wires all over the place, albeit hidden most of the time. If you discover round-pin plugs and sockets in your house you should consider rewiring completely, as the system is usually unsuitable for modern requirements. The danger is that to avoid the expense of fitting a new system, people try to add on to the old one with 13 amp sockets; they then fit a bigger piece of fuse wire to handle the increased current and as a result run the risk of the cable catching fire because of overload. This is definitely not recommended.

Figure 19.

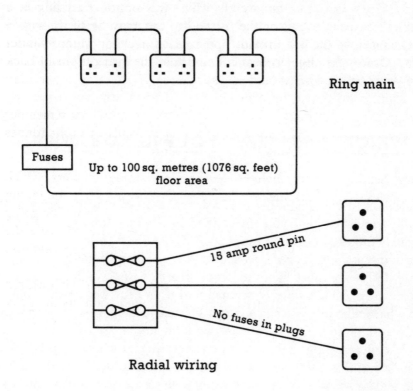

Ring main

Fuses

Up to 100 sq. metres (1076 sq. feet)
floor area

15 amp round pin

No fuses in plugs

Radial wiring

If your house has been wired since 1947, the system is likely to be of
the ring main variety; in this instance a cable comes out of the fuse box,
goes round the sockets on one floor and back into the fuse box (see Figure
19 for comparison with a radial circuit); lighting and large appliances
have separate circuits and fuses. The number of ring mains you have will
depend on the number of floors in your property and the floor area of
each. The maximum floor area one ring main can service is 100 sq metres
(119² sq yards). One of the great benefits of this system is that you can
add extra sockets (spurs) to the existing circuit. Generally speaking, ring
mains are more popular because they are easier and cheaper to install,
and the chances of overloading the system are pretty remote.

There is, in fact, no legal requirement to update an existing electrical
system – this is at present a totally unregulated industry – but you
should of course do it for your own protection. So if you are in any
doubt as to the acceptability of your present system you can either ask
your local electricity company or a private local contractor (possibly

subcontracted via your builder) to come and carry out a full electrical survey. They can tell you exactly what you've got, then advise on whether you need to rewire and/or add to the capacity of the system, depending upon the condition of the existing wiring and your requirements. One of the major benefits of completely rewiring is that you can have your sockets where you want them.

WHICH JOBS FIRST? YOUR RENOVATION FLOW CHART

In addition to understanding the basic make-up of your property, it is equally important that you understand in advance the order of tasks normally followed during a renovation. Quite apart from holding your own in discussions, it could even save you money by highlighting areas where delays are most likely to occur. Needless to say, time is always money where builders are concerned and if you can anticipate a delay with a particular job, you can have an alternative lined up so that nobody needs to stand idle. Obviously, no two renovations are the same – you may be concentrating on just one room or gutting the whole property. But regardless of this, there is most definitely a correct order of works that a good builder will observe and the various stages are normally as follows:

Dismantling and demolition

- clear the property of furniture and carpets, etc.
- isolate and protect any areas not having works done to them, particularly to protect from dust.
- fit supports to any loadbearing walls/partitions/floors which are to be altered or demolished (these are called 'temporary works' and may require the advice of a structural engineer).
- remove all redundant internal walls/partitions/electrics/plumbing/ fittings and leave the structure clear for further inspection.

Inspection

Now the builder will be able to see what needs to be done (as opposed to what you have requested) and if there are any unforeseen complications such as woodworm. It is at this point that the contingency element of your budget will probably be put to work and you may have to agree further works (in writing). There are almost always unexpected costs – and it isn't necessarily the builder trying to increase his profit margin! Many buildings (especially old ones constructed before modern building regulations) reveal faults when the 'insides' of the building are exposed. Common jobs at this stage are:

- timber treatment to floors, roof and stairs for woodworm and dry rot
- putting in damp-proof course (which involves taking plaster off the surrounding wall area)
- cleaning/re-lining chimneys if they are to be re-used.

Rebuilding and reconstruction

At this stage the builder is aiming to put back the fabric of the house to conform with:

1. the new layout;
2. current building regulations (which will involve the Local Authority Building Control Officer).

The scope of the work is wide-ranging and encompasses:

Construction
- laying the foundations for any new building, e.g. an extension
- constructing the footings of any new brick wall, up to and including damp-proof course
- digging trenches for services (either as a replacement or as a result of new building)
- laying drains, manholes, etc.
- starting to build up any new external walls, incorporating door and window frames, waste pipes, etc.
- repointing and stitching (repairing) old walls
- creating all necessary internal partitioning, ceilings and walls and putting in RSJs, etc., where necessary
- laying new or replacement floor joists, subfloors and stairs
- all roofing work, i.e. laying rafters, felt, tiles and fitting loft insulation
- external pipes, i.e. drainpipes and guttering installed

Services (whichever applicable)
This stage is often referred to as the 'first fix', and encompasses anything that subsequently gets covered by plastering, rendering or floorboarding:

- electricity
  - fitting the electricity meter box and fuse board back box
  - cutting chases (grooves) in internal walls for conduits, pipes and cables
  - laying electric cables for lighting, appliances such as cookers and power sockets
- telephone
  - laying the telephone lines and back boxes
- gas
  - installing the gas meter box
  - fitting pipework for gas boiler or gas cooker
- plumbing and water
  - installing cold water pipes from cold water tank for baths, basins, WCs, showers, etc.
  - installing cold water pipes direct from mains for domestic drinking water
  - installing pipes from hot water cylinder for kitchen and bathroom appliances
  - installing soil pipes
- central heating (for a normal radiator system)
  - fit pipes from boiler, expansion tank and for radiators

Finishings

At this point the property begins to take on a more finished look as the builder:

- renders and paints external walls (where applicable)
- plasterboards/plasters internal walls, partitions and ceilings. (These are often referred to as 'wet trades')
- lays floorboards

The 'Second Fix'

- installing the cold water tank and connecting to mains supply
- installing the hot water cylinder/immersion heater with pipe from cold water storage tank
- connecting waste pipes from baths, basins and WCs to soil pipes and gullies
- installing sanitary fittings, e.g. baths, basins, showers, toilets and

bidets and connecting to hot and cold water supply and to waste pipes
- installing expansion tank and connecting to mains supply
- installing boiler with connection from expansion tank
- installing radiators and connecting to feed pipes, testing and balancing the heating system
- building fitted units for kitchen, bathrooms and bedrooms
- fitting and connecting kitchen appliances, e.g. cookers and refrigerators
- other appliances, e.g. washing machines, tumble driers, etc., installed and connected to supply
- fitting power points and light fittings
- glazing windows (if not delivered pre-glazed) and fitting window catches and locks
- tiling walls
- hanging doors and fixing door handles, doorlocks, kick plates and letter plates
- fitting skirting boards, architraves, cornices, mouldings, etc.
- laying floor finishes (tiles, flagstones, etc.) and/or sanding floors
- fitting banister rails and staircase

Decorations

The final touches to your property are:
- undercoats and wall/woodwork preparations
- paint on walls, ceilings, woodwork
- wallpaper or fabric hanging
- fixing vanity shelving, loo roll holders and towel rings, etc.
- curtain tracks and poles fitted

Note: some decorators will put on the first coat of paint at the 'finishings' stage, so that there are no bald spots behind radiators, etc.

Furnishings

- carpets fitted
- curtains, blinds and light fittings hung
- telephones plugged in
- pictures, mirrors and furniture arranged.

A very useful exercise would be to plot your own specification against this table, just so that you know what the sequence of works is likely to be.

COMMON CAUSES OF DELAY

Contrary to what your friends and fellow renovators might have you believe, delays are not inevitable where building work is involved. Of course, there are always going to be some problems that you cannot anticipate and have to work around, but the truth is that there are just as many if not more that you can avoid with a bit of thought and planning.

The unavoidables

These really boil down to:

Weather
There is not much you can do if the elements send the great gale (remember 1987) the day after you have taken the roof off – as it did with us – but you should if possible choose the spring and summer months for any work likely to involve construction and/or the exterior of the property, e.g. digging trenches, laying foundations, building walls, roof work, fitting new doors and windows, guttering, etc. Painting is always tricky – remember that April and May can be wet months. A lot of painters favour October. But it goes without saying that if the work is urgent you cannot afford to wait for a sunny day and should just get on with it. Overall, don't get too worked up about the weather. Builders have to earn their living throughout the year and are fairly immune to it.

Sickness
It is up to the builder to get the job done within the time stated in your agreement (see Chapter Three) and to organise the appropriate manpower to fulfil this agreement. But that doesn't really help if he is a small business and hence the 'key person', in which case you just have to accept that progress may be delayed for a period. And be wary of

accepting someone in his place if you are not familiar with the standard of the deputy's work – it is better to wait than have the job badly done.

Delay in supply of materials

You should find out before the job starts if any of the materials are on long lead times; kitchen units can take weeks, whereas bricks can often be delivered the next day. The builder should of course have alternative sources of supply. Failing that, discuss the possibility of using different materials, but only after you have understood and approved any accompanying changes in the price quoted and assessed any planning and building regulations implications.

Surprise additions to the building spec

There shouldn't be too many of these if the initial inspection has been carried out property. But it none the less makes sense to make a mental allowance for problems such as damp or rot; I say mental allowance, because you don't need to tell the builder about it (unless you have serious grounds for suspecting the problem exists). If it is just a precautionary thought, he might relax because he knows that there is a bit of time in hand. You, on the other hand, want to make sure that this time is only used if absolutely necessary and for emergencies.

Delays that needn't be

Happily, this is the larger category and most often involves:

Official permissions

We have already looked at this in Chapter Four. Your main considerations will be planning permission and building regulations approval. Remember that you have to allow time for drawing up the application in addition to the 2–3 months it can take to be approved. Any amendments or appeals will add further to your schedule. At the risk of being over-cautious, allow six months for this part of the renovation process, i.e. six months before you actually want work to start. Utilities might also require significant periods of notice (6–8 weeks) – especially if you want a service laid on.

The client changing their mind

Now, I know that you wouldn't dream of such a thing ... but if you do want to make alterations once work is in progress, accept that this can have ramifications in terms of time and especially of cost. If the job has been well planned in the first place (go back to Chapter One!) it won't be necessary. But if you simply cannot avoid/resist making further changes to the original scheme, be prepared for the following:

- possible expense arising from the cancellation of a previous order to a supplier or sub-contractor
- extra time to obtain your new requirements
- extra time to provide a quotation for the new works
- extra time to place new orders and await delivery
- other trades being held up while these changes take place (especially if the work involves a first fix)
- extra time and expense to carry out the works (this is where the builder will really punish you)

Sequence problems

Obviously, if certain materials haven't arrived, e.g. kitchen tiles, the builder should have some other task to turn to rather than just stand scratching his head!

Put like that, none of the above seems worth it, does it? It's far simpler to know what you want and stick to it. If nothing else, it will concentrate your mind wonderfully when choosing those new floor tiles. And on the subject of knowing what you want, you can save time, money and aggravation by presenting your builder with as detailed a brief as possible. Read on.

CHAPTER SIX

Down to Detail

A large part of your success in dealing with any contractor is to brief them in as much detail as possible, not only in writing, but preferably with diagrams as well. A good spec is essential, but the written word is unfortunately still open to interpretation. Simple diagrams, however, can leave the recipient in no doubt as to what you want, and you should be working on these while the spec is being agreed, so that the finished diagrams reflect faithfully the contents of your written list of works. It's a relatively small effort on your part which can prevent mistakes and thus avoid further cost. To do this you have to think through the layout and fine detail of each room – an area which first-time renovators often neglect. Well organised rooms take a lot of planning and you should leave yourself plenty of time for this part of the renovation process. After all, you are going to have to live with the result, not the builder.

THE FUNDAMENTALS OF ROOM PLANNING

Every room in the house merits a bit of thought to maximise its potential and the key issues are normally circulation space and the position of heating/lighting fixtures. But without doubt, the most complicated rooms and those in which people most often make mistakes, are the kitchen and the bathroom(s):

The kitchen

I should start by saying that many kitchen suppliers offer excellent computerised planning services which they normally perform free of charge in the hope that you will buy one of their kitchens. You just take the measurements of your kitchen to their showroom, they feed it all into a computer and out come various design permutations. Of course, it's a bit sneaky to take advantage of this offer if you have no intention of buying the range, but if inspiration fails you completely it's a great way of getting some ideas . . . and you may just fall in love with a kitchen while you are there! Otherwise, here are a few planning basics to help you make the best use of the resources available:

Circulation

1. The golden rule in kitchens, regardless of their size, is one of ergonomics, i.e. how easy it is to work in them. Always try to stick to the triangle rule and have your cooker, fridge and sink as nearly as possible in a triangle formation (see Figure 20), so that you can move freely and quickly between these work-intensive areas. You will find that this is much less time-consuming than if the appliances are in a straight line. Also try to have a utility surface next to the cooker and the sink. If you are likely to have more than one person cooking at any one time, place the cooker away from the microwave, so that different activities can take place without interference.

2. Depending on the size of your kitchen, keep a separate area reserved for seating away from the main cooking activity, mainly to avoid collisions with the cook! This becomes especially important if you entertain in the kitchen and want to create a quiet corner, or if the kitchen is used for homework or watching TV, etc.

Layout

1. Make sure that all equipment can be stored close to where it is to be used and is easily accessible, especially if it is used on a regular basis. Don't forget that you can fit cupboards and drawers with special space-saving storage devices, e.g. carousels in corner cupboards, deep mesh drawers for saucepans, adjustable shelves within units.

2. Try to put the sink by a window, if only to make your life more interesting while doing the washing up!

3. Try to have the cooker against an outside wall, to allow for an

Figure 20. Triangle Formation for Kitchens

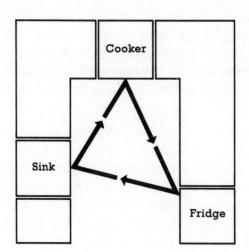

extractor (a building regs requirement). Remember that cookers can come as a single unit incorporating oven, grill, hob and even micro-wave or as a separate oven and hob.

4. In narrow kitchens be wary of wall-cupboards, which will not only emphasise the feeling of claustrophobia but be quite difficult to open without knocking yourself out! Consider open shelving.

5. Check the height of wall units – too high and the space will become redundant if you can't easily reach it; too low and it will inhibit your use of work surfaces beneath.

Appliances and fittings

1. Remember the following basic items as you plan your kitchen: cooker/hob, oven, microwave, fridge/freezer, washing machine, sink, fan, cabinets, larder, broom cupboard.

2. Unless you actually want to cultivate the 'lived in' look, try to streamline the kitchen wherever possible and disguise appliances within units.

3. Always put in more work surfaces than you think you may need,

especially since toasters, microwaves and kettles have a knack of invading space.

4. This is a personal opinion, but tiled worksurfaces tend to look grubby as the grouting picks up dirt and they don't strike me as terribly hygienic. A good worksurface should be strong, heat and stain resistant; laminates, granite and marble are all possibilities and some of the new synthetics, such as Corian, are particularly hardwearing.

5. Choose flooring for its practical qualities as well as looks. Vinyl is warmer underfoot and you are less likely to break things if they drop, but it can be damaged by heat. Ceramic tiles and flagstones are very attractive, especially in a rustic setting, but must be set properly to prevent 'rocking' and should also be sealed to prevent staining. Wood strip floors can look wonderful and actually improve with age, but also need sealing. Carpet is of course very warm, but not necessarily very hygienic for a kitchen.

6. Don't overdose on appliances; dishwashers are labour saving, but need a lot of crockery to make the wash worth while.

Space savers

1. If your kitchen is small, consider moving the washing machine/ tumble drier and freezer to another room, preferably near by; this also removes the nuisance of excessive condensation in your cooking area. If you are short of space consider a combined washer/drier.

2. If you are really stuck for room, consider leaving out a floor unit so that a chair can be tucked in the gap and the work surface above can double as a breakfast bar. If you don't want to sacrifice the cupboard space, there are units available which incorporate pull-out table tops.

3. Remember that most base units are built to standard sizes, usually 900 mm (35½ inches) high and 650 mm (25½ inches) deep. If you are vertically or horizontally challenged, or have a very narrow kitchen, consider custom-built furniture. If that is beyond your budget, buy normal sized units and have the builder cut them down – but first check with him that it is going to be viable. NB. if you are buying a kitchen 'off the shelf', and want to cut down the units, make sure that it comes flat packed; some kitchens come as ready-glued units and it is that much more difficult for the builder to alter them.

4. Buy small-sized appliances wherever possible – you can, for example, buy dishwashers that fit under the drainer of a sink unit.

Lighting

1. You need clear, strong light to work by, e.g. halogens or strip lighting, and a softer light, e.g. a pendant fitting, for your eating area. Work surfaces can be lit by fittings built into wall units, into the cooker hood or just positioned above the sink.

2. Make the best use of any natural light that is available; an east-facing window is a good place to have a breakfast table because it will catch the early morning sun.

Bathrooms

Circulation

1. Again, this is the big buzz word, and an understandable problem given that the average British bathroom measures just 1.5 m × 2 m (5 feet × 6½ feet). Make sure that you can use the loo without falling into the bath and get up from it without kneecapping yourself on the basin. I once stayed in a hotel room where the loo was no more than 152 mm (6 inches) from the opposite wall, forcing the user to sit sideways on – quite the highspot of the holiday! Similarly, you need to be able to stand back from the basin when you bend down to wash your face/hair/teeth, etc., and perhaps to be able to kneel in front of the bath to wash a baby, etc. The official recomendations are 700 mm (27½ inches) square in front of a WC, 700 mm × 1000 mm × 39 inches (width) in front of a basin and a similar floor area outside a shower for drying yourself and opening the hinged screen. If the existing arrangement of fittings isn't satisfactory, see if you can have them repositioned – although this might mean long runs of pipe being boxed in.

Layout

1. Decide whether or not you actually want the loo in the bathroom. Some people prefer not to. For others, especially those with only one bathroom/loo and several people in the family, it has to be in a separate room for logistical reasons (depending upon the position of the soil pipe).

2. If you need more space consider moving a door, radiator or airing cupboard.

3. Avoid putting the bath under a window. If you have a shower attachment the glass will get mucky every time it is used, not to mention puddles on the window sill.

4. Basins can go under windows – so long as you don't need a mirror above and don't splash too much!

5. The toilet normally has to go against an outside wall to allow for the soil pipe.

6. Consider corner baths for making the most of difficult spaces.

Fittings

1. Decide upon your priorities. Normally, fittings include a bath, basin and WC, although you may want a shower and bidet as well. There should also be room to store towels and toiletries.

2. If you are planning shower doors, make sure the ceiling is high enough, because it is difficult to install a 2.4 m (8 ft) shower door in a room with a 1.8 m (6 ft) high ceiling – don't laugh, I actually know someone who tried it.

3. Remember that cast-iron baths are very heavy (not to mention the water that sits in them) and may need extra floor support if above ground floor level.

4. Choose practical fittings, e.g. baths with low sides for elderly people and children or wall mounted washbasins if you want to make floor cleaning easier.

5. Tiles can be very classy but also horribly expensive. Cut down on the amount you need by tiling just the areas which come into contact with water most frequently, i.e. the bath and basin. The rest of the room can be plastered and painted or wallpapered. Consider using the special fungicide paints that are now on the market – they can be very effective against mould growth.

6. Decide what type of shower you need. In a low pressure area it might be a good idea to go for a special power shower.

Lighting

1. Bathroom lighting is fraught with danger. Most important, all fittings should be totally enclosed so that water cannot hit the bulb, and socket outlets should not be installed unless they are the recommended type of shaver socket. It is part of the IEE recommended code of practice that your light switch has either to be outside the bathroom or on a pull cord inside. It all depends on how paranoid you are about people turning the light off from outside while you are in the bath! Portable electrical appliances should never be used in the bathroom.

Ventilation

1. Don't forget ventilation. Fans are a good idea, especially when switched on by a humidity stat, which operates only when the humidity in the room reaches a certain level.

THE MOST COMMON OVERSIGHTS

For those inexperienced in renovation works it is very easy to trip up on the small but vital details. In particular watch out for the following:

Choice of lighting

That is, the position and number of wall lights and switches. I have a theory, born of experience, which is that by the time 'renovators' come to decide upon light fittings they are so punch drunk that they settle for whatever seems simplest – usually a budget system of one central ceiling rose and one light switch. This is a big mistake. Not only is good lighting essential for your eyesight, but the inconvenience and expense of making subsequent alterations should encourage you to do it properly the first time. Ideally your property should possess the following types of lighting:

1. 'all purpose' lighting, i.e. that which provides an acceptable level of visibility in each room. Often these lights are centrally hung.

2. 'service' lighting – strong overhead lights for full illumination of working surfaces, e.g. desks, kitchens, worktops, etc.

3. 'living' lighting, i.e. your mood lighting; a softer, more indirect light used for atmosphere as much as illumination, and which can give a completely different feel to a room without involving any decorating changes. This might include wall lights, cabinet lighting, table and standard lamps, etc. Remember dimmer switchers too – very effective.

4. 'safety' lighting – illumination for any particular blackspots, e.g. dark corners, difficult steps, etc.

Quality of light

There are basically three types to choose from:

1. Incandescent bulbs, i.e. the ones most of us are used to, which give off a warm soft light, are reasonably cheap to buy and consequently used for general-purpose lighting.

2. Fluorescent strip lights, which give off a clear blue/white light and tend to be more effective in kitchens and places where there are work surfaces.

3. Low and mains voltage halogen lighting, which gives off a very pure white light and is good for any area where focus is needed, e.g. reading lamps and work surfaces. The fittings are, however, much more expensive than normal light bulbs. Mains voltage halogen light is very strong and tends to be used for floodlighting large areas, .e.g. in the garden. Lower wattage halogen light is normally used indoors. NB. Neither fluorescent nor halogen lights can be dimmed.

Position and height of lighting

This is particularly important in those rooms where you want to read or work.

1. For kitchen work surfaces and serving areas consider having strip lights concealed under the cupboards (ideally 370 – 450 mm/$14\frac{1}{2}$ – $17\frac{3}{4}$ inches above the surface). This will provide a focused pool of light and overcome the problem of shadows caused by overhead lighting.

2. In bedrooms you might want a reading light either side of the bed;

the recommended height for this fitting is 750 mm (29½ inches) above the mattress – to ensure that the light shines directly over your head.

3. In bathrooms you should illuminate mirrors with fittings 600 – 750 mm (23½ – 29½ inches) apart either side or else opt for a strip light or all round 'Hollywood' style bulb lighting – but remember that the fitting must always be suitable for use in bathrooms to be safe.

Position of light switches

1. Think about where you will find it most convenient to switch the light on – and off! The two most common problem areas are bedrooms and stairs. Most of us don't want to get out of a cosy bed to turn off the light, so the obvious answer is to have another switch by the bed. With stairways, the emphasis is on safety and you should always have light switches at both the top and bottom.

2. Make sure your switches are at a comfortable height. Too low or too high on the wall and they will be a constant irritation. Just reach out and see what is right for you (and other members of the household) – 1.45 metres (4 feet 9 inches) above floor level is normal.

Position and number of electrical sockets

1. The golden rule is to install about 50 per cent more than you think you are going to need. Too few sockets will put a constraint upon where you can move your furniture and lamps, whereas if you have several 'spares', it won't matter if some are lost behind cupboards, etc. You should be particularly extravagant in the kitchen, since we all tend to acquire electrical clutter (food blenders, babies' food warmers, kettles, etc.) all of which needs to be plugged in. The Electrical Installation Industry Liaison Committee (EIILC) recommends a minimum number of electrical sockets (of the twin switched type) for the average house (see Table on page 130).

It is likely, however, that you will need even more than this. So make a list of all your appliances and where in the house you are likely to want to plug them in. Then make another list of all the appliances you might acquire over the next few years. Consider whether they will need to occupy a socket full time or can 'share' with another appliance. To help you, here are a few common items

129

Kitchen	4	Landing/stairs	1
Living room	6	Hall	1
Dining room	3	(for vacuum cleaner, if nothing else!)	
Double bedroom	4	Garage	2
Single bed-sitting room	4	Store/workroom	1
Single bedroom/teenager's room	3		

which may need the use of a socket: fridge, washing machine, tumble drier, dishwasher, foodmixer, toaster, kettle, cooker, iron, microwave, lamp, vacuum cleaner, television, video, radio, hi-fi, sewing machine, hair dryer, teasmade, razor (socket), heated trouser press, electric blanket. See what I mean about accumulation?

2. Use double sockets wherever possible. They really are most practical and well worth the small additional cost.

3. Make sure your sockets are well above ground level, say 300 – 400 mm (12 – 16 inches). Not only will this protect them in case of flooding, but will prevent the cables being caught up in chair legs and vacuum cleaners, etc.

4. It will save time and money if you can have sockets installed back to back in adjacent rooms.

Position of radiators

1. In an average brick-and-block-built house you will normally find the radiator under the window, for two reasons:

- Firstly because the poor heat efficiency of the house will be such that a fairly large radiator is needed and to put it anywhere else in the room would clutter up an area of wall which might have a better use.
- Secondly, because the radiator helps to alleviate condensation on the window (although, of course, you should be seeking to cure condensation, not just alleviate it). The disadvantage of this set up is that heat goes straight out of the window, even more so when curtains are drawn. And to make matters worse, most windows are positioned on outside walls where the heat loss is even greater.

So, the moral is that radiators do *not* have to go under windows (especially if you have double glazing). In theory you can put them anywhere you have some dead wall space, e.g. behind the door, so long as the air can flow around it freely to take the warmth to the rest of the room. And give some thought to the shape of the room. If it is long and thin it may be better to have two small radiators, one at either end of the room, instead of just one large one.

2. Remember also that radiator covers will reduce heat emission by 5 – 10 per cent, so allow for that if you intend to use them.

3. Consider using thermostatic valves, which will turn the radiator off when the room reaches a pre-set temperature. They can be fitted on to any radiator and are obviously cost/energy savers.

Position and number of telephone points

1. Again, always put in more than you think you might need. You cannot always predict how many telephones you will accumulate and in which rooms they will prove most useful. Remember, however, that there is a limit to the loading you are allowed to put on the line, measured in RENs (Ringer Equivalent Number) and this is currently 4 for each household; so you have to check the REN number of each telephone, answerphone or fax to make sure that you haven't exceeded your allowance. If you have, the cordless 'phone is an alternative.

Ceiling height

1. If you happen to be altering your ceiling height it is worth noting that it is not mandatory but sensible to make sure that upstairs ceilings are 2.2 m (7 feet 2½ inches) high and downstairs 2.35 m (7 feet 8½ inches) high.

Doorways

1. For obvious reasons of safety, no door should open out on to a passageway (unless it has toughened glass).

2. External doors should open in such a way that the wind can blow them shut, so that they don't get ripped off their hinges. For energy conservation reasons, avoid having external doors facing the prevailing wind; alternatively, fit a porch.

3. Doors leading into bathrooms and bedrooms should open in such a way that they retain as much of your privacy as possible. For example, if the bath or loo are on the right hand side as you enter, have the door open from left to right, so that they and anybody using them are not the first thing on view as you open the door!

Circulation space

1. Whatever the size of your house, there should be a good balance between room space and circulation space, i.e. you need room to sit, eat, etc., but also adequate means of moving between rooms. As a rule of thumb you should allocate approximately 20 per cent of floor area as passageway. Make sure there is enough space to move large items of furniture in and out of the property; you don't want to become one of the many who get wedged in the stairwell with their wardrobe.

Security

1. This is often neglected and is an area where for a relatively small amount of money you can save a lot of heartache. All windows, but especially those on the ground floor at the back of the house (which includes patios), should have window locks fitted; pay particular attention to windows that can be accessed from flat roof areas and soil/rainwater pipes. Consider window bars on skylights and a bolt on the trap door to the loft. Garages and gardens sheds should have padlocks and something on the windows to prevent people seeing what equipment is stored inside. The front and back door should also have locks and in the case of the former, a door chain and door-viewer as well. For outside areas, lights with in-built sensors are excellent, as they turn on automatically when they detect body heat.

HOW TO DRAW UP DETAILED ROOM
PLANS

A good room plan will not only help the builder understand what you want, but even more important, will act as an instruction for the man on site. Remember that the builder will be delegating to electricians, plumbers and kitchen fitters, etc. If the builder is uncertain as to exactly where you want that light fitting, the electrician will simply get an even more diluted version of the instruction. With the best intentions in the world he might then be forced to make an intelligent guess as to where to fix the light – and you can be sure that it won't be where you intended! Alternatively, he just stops work and wastes time, which in turn costs you money.

With a diagram, however, you have bypassed the 'builder to work-man' stage in the chain of command, demonstrated clearly what you want directly to the person who is actually going to do the work and have probably avoided delays, mistakes and, ultimately, further cost. Equally important, you have not gone over the builder's head – you simply give him two copies of the plans, one of which is then passed on to the workmen.

Unless your room plans are very complicated and require the input of an architect (see Chapter Two), a simple sketch with key will suffice. Simple, however, does not mean lacking in detail. The absolute golden rule with these plans is that they must show exactly where you want things put: don't leave anything to the builder's imagination. This doesn't have to be to scale, although it helps enormously to give accurate measurements. Both for the sake of clarity, and because each fitter should have his own diagram, I normaly draw up separate plans for electrics and plumbing, e.g. bathroom fittings (see Figure 21). Supplement those diagrams with further information, particularly:

- The height above ground level of power sockets
- The height above ground level for light switches
- The exact position for telephone and television points
- The length of drop for ceiling lights

In other words, make it crystal clear where you want your fixtures and fittings.

Kitchen plans are especially important, because most people have fitted units of some kind and the general idea is that they should do just that – fit, in addition to incorporating all sorts of appliances. So whether you are marking up a page for your builder's use or to take to a kitchen planner, observe the following:

1. Use squared paper. Draw in the kitchen length and width, marking doorways, windows, serving hatches, electrical points, water, waste and gas pipes and if applicable, radiator pipe(s) and radiator(s).

Figure 21. Room Plans for Electrician

Key

X = Ceiling light   LS = Light switch

□ = Power Point   DLS = Double light switch

▥ = Double power point   LS (d) = Light switch with dimmer

TP = Telephone point   TVP = Television point

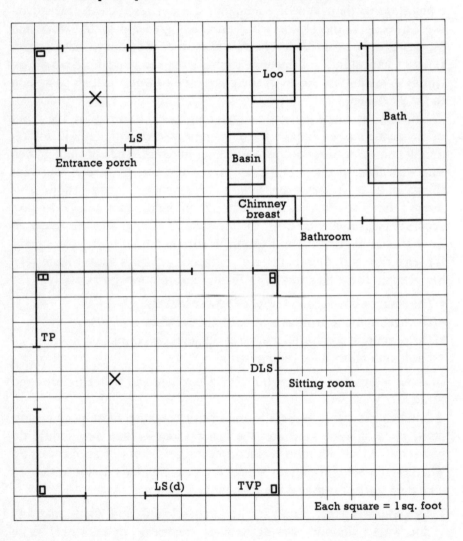

Each square = 1 sq. foot

2. Make a note of which way doors and windows open.

3. Make a note of the height of the ceiling and the distance between the floor and bottom edge of the window.

4. If your kitchen is particularly narrow, measure up the ideal depth of unit needed (allowing adequate circulation space for yourself), just in case you want to buy standard units and cut them down. Another tip: wall cupboards are invariably shallower than floor units, and are often perfect as a floor unit for a narrow kitchen. All you need is a plinth at the bottom to raise them a few inches from the floor and it could save you the bother of having to cut floor units to fit.

If you have followed my advice this far, you should not only be well versed in how the renovation works should progress but be backed up by good documentation as well. Now you have to put the theory into practice and make sure that the builder keeps to his side of the bargain.

CHAPTER SEVEN

Staying in Control

You may wonder if this chapter is necessary. Not only do you have a proper written agreement with the builder, but you have also provided him with brilliantly clear diagrams! What could possibly go wrong? Well, in the real world, a piece of paper does not guarantee that the builder is going to do what you want, and it is therefore much better to have site meetings as you go along, to discuss changes to the spec, delays with materials and so on, than to have a confrontation at the end of the job. Other safety measures are to have a list of items against which you can check the builder's workmanship and to at least be aware of some of the less honest practices builders can indulge in. Your best tactic, however, is simply to exploit your builder's Achilles heel – that of administration; a builder who spends adequate time on his paperwork is a rare creature indeed. So when the building works get going, what you lack in knowledge you can make up for in control simply by being meticulous about site meeting notes, progress reports and general documentation. But don't forget that your relationship should ideally be one based on co-operation, not conflict – and there are several practical things you can do to make the builder's life easier and the renovation process smoother.

SITE MEETINGS

The principle is much the same regardless of your geographical location and circumstances:

1. If you are living in the property while it is being renovated you may think you can monitor progress on a constant basis. The danger is that you interfere with the daily routine by chatting with the workmen, or worse still, make random requests to do little extras. This is the fastest way to incur extra cost because nothing is for free; the builder will make a careful mental note and use it as evidence if you query the (enlarged) final bill. You also run the risk of the workmen thinking that you are just checking up on them, which is guaranteed to cause bad feeling. The answer is to stay out of their way (somewhat easier if you are out at work during the day) as much as possible and only deal with one person, the builder. Let him handle his men.

2. If you are not occupying the property it is even more imperative to have regular site meetings. Our cottage was 240 kilometres (150 miles) away but we still made the 480-kilometre (300-mile) round trip on a weekly basis, and I feel that it was definitely worth while. A lot can happen in a week, especially during the demolition and reconstruction stages. You might not otherwise discover those York flagstones beneath the old cracked concrete floor or the Victorian kitchen range built into the fire breast, but the builder will, and they might well be whisked away if you are not there to say otherwise.

Whichever situation you are in, the procedure is the same. Work out a timetable for site meetings. This may be on a weekly or fortnightly basis, regardless of the work done, or it may be linked to individual stages completed, e.g. plumbing, electrics, etc. Be disciplined about these meetings: turn up with a copy of the specification, a notebook, pen and an understanding of what you expect to have been done. There are several things you want to get out of each site meeting:

- To monitor progress – tick items off the specification as they are completed, which will also help you identify them for payment.
- To reach agreement on what is meant to be finished by the time of the next meeting – then everyone is aware of the short-term goals. If your builder is really clued up he will have produced a timetable of works, which will have facilitated this process enormously (see Figure 22). I can't pretend that this is normal practice but you can of course ask for one to be drawn up when you award the contract.
- To make detailed notes of any changes to the original specification. These may be at your own instigation or at the builder's suggestion.

Figure 22. Part of a typical Timetable of Work

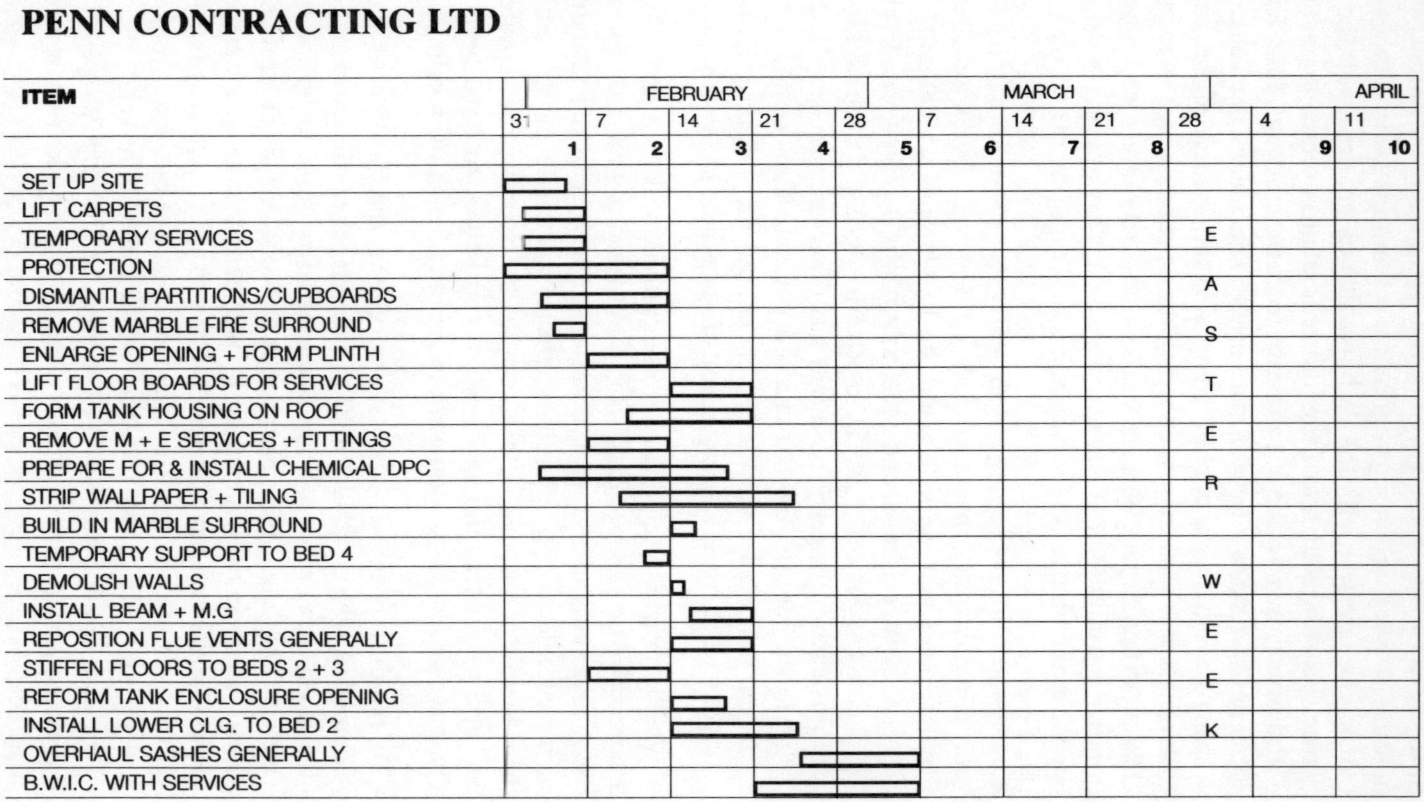

PENN CONTRACTING LTD

Straight after the meeting you should sit down and write up your notes. The purpose of doing this is to confirm what was agreed with the builder, particularly any changes relating to materials, cost and timing. You should make these notes as comprehensive as possible – it's always going to be the point you fail to record that becomes contentious! And make it a requirement of payment that any changes are unauthorised until agreed in writing (see section on contracts in Chapter Three). Send a copy of those minutes to the builder immediately after the meeting, faxing them if possible. The more documentation you have the better – and the less room there is for confusion and misinterpretation. It also puts the onus on the builder to come back to you with any queries he might have.

ASSESSING THE BUILDER'S WORK

Managing a successful property renovation is very much about staying in control of the operation and, as we have just seen, regular site meetings are essential to ensure that the project is completed on time and within budget. But you could and should go one step further than that and devise a series of ongoing 'quality control' inspections. No one is expecting you to become an instant expert on building techniques, but there are a number of simple checks that anyone can make to assess the competence and professionalism of the contractor. Not only will this knowledge gain you some respect from the builder but it will also mean that you have some understanding of:

The materials used

A common trick is to shortchange the customer on materials because most people don't understand the significance of using, say, a 9 mm ($\frac{3}{8}$ inch) plasterboard when a 1 cm ($\frac{1}{2}$ inch) would be preferable. The builder, however, knows that the 9 mm ($\frac{3}{8}$ inch) is much cheaper and you are unlikely to spot the difference!

Correct building practice

For example, the correct sequence for laying a floor. Here it is not so much the materials which are expensive but the amount of time it takes to do the job properly. Again, the average person wouldn't know if one or more of the stages had been left out and the builder can take advantage of this fact.

'Hidden works'

The problem here is that most clients only inspect the renovation when it is completely finished and most builders will make sure that superficially it looks pretty good. But of course by then it is impossible for the customer to see what has been done underneath and it is often there that the real problems lurk (e.g. damp), waiting to surface long after the builder has gone with your money! However, if you appear to know a bit about correct building practice, this is much less likely to happen.

You may rightly point out that this is what a specification is for, to agree detail on procedure, materials and cost. And it is. But in the real world what people say/write and what they do are often two different things. What is more, these practices are not confined to the few cowboy builders, they are quite common and sometimes considered a legitimate way of bumping up the profit, but you can stay one step ahead by investing in a little knowledge. Keep an eye on the following:

Demolition works

The first system of checks should actually take place during demolition work. This is by far the most tricky part of your checking procedure and the most technical. The problem you have in most renovations is that the builder must start by 'stripping out', i.e. taking back the fabric of the house in preparation for new works. It is at this stage that nasty surprises can come to light, such as rot and damp, that the original surveyor's report might not have thrown up. You have to make sure that the right amount of stripping takes place; not enough and faults remain hidden, too much and the builder can create unnecessary work. In other words, you want to make sure that any suggested changes to the original specification are legitimate. Your best bet is to invite the local building inspector to come and take a look. The frustrated architect in him will be only too pleased to advise you on how far to take back the fabric of the property. He can also then guide you on the following:

Walls

Here you are checking for dampness, and the soundness of plaster. Any areas of loose plaster should be taken off to expose the brick/stone underneath. If what you find is dry and has a good damp-proof course, it shouldn't need any further work. If it is wet, you may well need to have a damp-proof course replaced or if there isn't one, have it fitted.

Windows, window sills, floorboards, joists, rafters

Here you want to see how sound the wood is. The simple test is to use a screwdriver to dig into the wood. Anything rotten will give way and have to be replaced. If the rot is localised it may be possible to cut into the wood and just replace a section. Otherwise the whole thing will have to be taken out.

Wiring

Have a close look at the wiring. Anything other than the new PVC type cable is not really acceptable and should be replaced. If you intend to add more electrical fittings you should agree to strip the whole lot out and start again rather than just tack bits on.

Plumbing

Many houses for renovation have either no central heating or a system that is woefully inadequate. You should particularly look out for leaks, bent and damaged pipes, and replace as necessary.

Roof

Inside the roof you should look out for leaks in the felt and outside, check the soundness of the tiles, lead flashing, ridges and hips. Flat roofs are slightly more tricky because there is no loft to inspect; remember that the standard life of a flat roof is 10–15 years, so be especially careful of any that are older than that. Check to see if the flashing is firm and tight, consider replacing any bits of asphalt which are blistered or lifting, look to see if there are excessive amounts of moss and algae growing on the roof and that the shingle is still giving even coverage of the roof area.

Structural works and first fix

Once the builder has started work to an agreed final specification, there is a whole series of points you can check as work progresses. This list is by no means comprehensive, but it will keep the builder on his toes! From the top then:

Roof

- Ideally a builder should use foil-backed plasterboard for ceilings beneath the roof; this limits the amount of moisture that can enter the roof area from the rooms below. But a polythene sheet with ordinary plasterboard is just as good.

- If possible, have a look at any work being done on the roof itself. The felt should be free of rips and tears, strips of felt should overlap to prevent gaps, and galvanised nails should be used when securing battens, to prevent corrosion.

Joists and rafters

- Any joist weakened by woodworm should be *completely* removed and replaced. If a timber is affected but is not of structural importance, it should at least be thoroughly treated. Don't be fobbed off with anything less.

- Dry rot is not to be taken lightly. All timber and masonry within a 1.2 – 1.8 metre (4 – 6 ft) radius of the affected area should be removed and all other timber in the house treated.

- Check that any damaged and/or weak timbers are being replaced. Again, your building inspector will probably be pleased to help monitor this work.

- Any timber which needs strengthening should be properly bolted to the new one. Watch out for builders who just nail them on – this is a purely cosmetic solution and doesn't strengthen anything.

- Look at replacement timbers. They should be 4 times the length of the piece they are replacing, to ensure that the load carried by the piece of timber is safely transferred to the replacement.

Walls

- If any bricklaying is being done, make sure that the mortar is sound. Scrape a metal nail across it after three days or so; if it is loose and 'fluffy', the builder hasn't used enough cement in the mix.

- If a cavity wall is being built, check that excess mortar hasn't dropped down the cavity. It if has, it will form a bridge between the outer and inner wall, prevent the damp-proof course from working and yes, you've guessed it, cause damp. By the way, this excess mortar is called 'snot' in the trade – strange but true!

- All bricks should be clean and free of grease or mud, otherwise any render that is applied to them will not be able to bond.

- A rather obvious one this, but walls should be vertical and flat and corners square (unless, of course, your house is of a certain age). This is especially important in kitchens, to ensure that your units fit snugly. Check with a spirit level and a piece of string.

Floors

The correct way to lay a concrete floor is to put down 100 mm (4 inches) of well-compacted hardcore, 50 mm (2 inches) of blinding sand on top of that, then a damp-proof membrane, followed by 100 – 150 mm (4 – 6 inches) of concrete and then a 50 mm (2 inch) layer of screed (a flooring sand-cement mix). At this point the floor is ready for the final floorcovering. Always check that:

- the blinding sand layer has been laid. Builders might try to leave this out to save time and money.

- any adjoining membrane sheets overlap by 500 mm (20 inches) or are taped, to prevent leakages.

- that when the membrane sheets are laid the builders don't puncture them with their boots or wheelbarrows – the blinding sand is there to reduce this risk.

- that the builder has actually removed the existing floor. A common trick is to paint the old floor with a bituminous sealer and then screed on top! Once again, if you only evaluate the floor when the nice new flagstones have been laid, you won't realise that the job hasn't been properly done.

Wiring

- All cables should run straight up or down from their backboxes (the metal boxes set into the wall behind power points and light switches) – usually down from power points and up from light switches. It is important that they run vertically, not diagonally, from the backboxes, so that you can gauge where it is safe to drill when subsequently hanging pictures, etc.

- For the same reason all cables should be protected by a channel or 'sheath' (either plastic or metal but the latter is preferable).

- Power and lighting cables should not share the same back box as the telephone, and should be one foot away from any aerial, to avoid pick-up. Telephone and electric cables should be 150 mm (6 inches apart).

- Check the plastic coating of cables to see if they are scored, cut or damaged. It is especially important to look for this after the plasterers have been as they use extremely sharp tools.

Plumbing

- Look at a few joints after they have been soldered. A good plumber will wipe away the excess flux (a soldering aid). If he doesn't, green deposits will form a day or two later which will eventually corrode the pipe.

- Ask whether lead-free solder is going to be used on your hot and cold pipes. I would insist that they are, for the obvious health reasons.

Second fix and final finishes

There are a lot of things you can check here:

Plasterboarding

- Take any piece of plasterboard on a ceiling or stud partition wall and push at it where it has been nailed. If it moves on the nail, this suggests that it hasn't been nailed tightly enough against the timber and the ceiling plaster will eventually fall from the area around the nail. In the trade this is called a 'popper'.

- Plasterboard is normally delivered with protective binding tape around the edge. This should always be removed before skimming to ensure that the plaster bonds well. Leaving it on is definitely a sign of indifferent workmanship.

- Check that the plasterboard isn't damaged and exposing the plaster within. If it is, you are guaranteed an imperfect surface when the plaster is applied.

- Make sure that the builder uses full-sized plasterboard sheets, not offcuts; your ceiling shouldn't look like a patchwork quilt. The boards should measure 8 × 4 ft or 6 × 3 ft (2.44 × 1.22m or 1.83 × 0.92m).

- As I mentioned above, a good builder will use 10 mm ($\frac{1}{2}$ inch) board for ceilings to provide the necessary strength and keep the ceiling flat. But they might try to substitute board of 9 mm ($\frac{3}{8}$ inch) because it is lighter and cheaper. Ask the builder to state the thickness in the specification.

- Check that all joints are covered with reinforcing scrim; scrim is a reinforcement that you tape to the edges of plasterboard immediately prior to skimming, to reduce the amount of cracking where plasterboards join.

- Electric back boxes in plasterboard should be firmly fixed. A sloppy fit will lead to a loose socket or switch.

Rendering – the pre-plaster layer

- Whether inside or outside the house, all external corners i.e. corners projecting into a space, should have 'render beads' (galvanised strips of mesh) to act as a reinforcement.

- The render itself should be applied in one or two coats. If external, waterproofer should be added. The second coat should be weaker than the first, to prevent cracking.

Skimming – the application of plaster

- Skimming should be done in 'sets' – the ceiling first, then one opposing pair of walls and lastly, the other pair. Doing the ceiling first prevents 'snot' on the walls.

- Run your fingers over the skimming. It should be smooth. If what you touch feels like a piece of braille, the plasterer hasn't done a good job. The only exception to this is when you want to apply emulsion, which needs a rougher surface to enable it to bond. Just shine a torch along the surface – all will be revealed.

- Look for water marks. These are pale patches found just after the plaster has dried. They suggest that the plasterer didn't make the wall

145

flat before putting on the plaster and although they may feel quite dry they will never set completely hard.

- Examine the corners of walls. They should be clean, smooth and without streaks, i.e. trowel marks.

Windows, external doors and window sills

- Windows and external doors should be secured to the adjoining wall with 'frame fixings' (little L-shaped bits of steel) every 230 – 305 mm (9 – 12 inches). Otherwise a determined thief could kick them in.

- A good builder will wrap a plastic damp-proof course around a window frame before fitting it into its opening. This will protect the wood from any wet in the wall and the visible plastic can be subsequently removed with a Stanley knife.

- Window sills should be securely fixed to stop them bowing through damp. Screws are more effective than nails. The same goes for skirting boards, architraves and door linings.

Floors

- If you are having new timber floors the builder should lay plastic sheeting over the floor to prevent water damage from rendering and skimming. I would hazard that a great deal of the builder's time is spent cleaning floors of muck which needn't have been there in the first place.

- If he hasn't already done it and if you aren't planning on having exposed floorboards, ask the builder to mark the floorboards (in felt tip pen) so that you can identify the position of pipes and cables running beneath; this will save a lot of time if you ever need to locate them for repair, etc.

Tiling

- Common sense this one, but all tiles should lie flat and the grout be evenly applied.

- In bathrooms you should check that only waterproof grout is used and in kitchens, that the grout is 'hygienically safe', i.e. that it does not contain any mercury-based fungicide; you obviously don't want anything containing mercury close to your drinking-water supply or food.

- Where tiles meet a bath edge, the builder should put in a sealer strip which goes up behind the tile and overlaps on to the rim of the bath; it is inevitable that your bath will move, even if only by a few millimetres, and when it does, rigid grout will crack and you will want to prevent water seeping up behind the tiles. Again, this is not something all builders do automatically, but it is a sign of good workmanship.

Kitchen units

- Most sinks come delivered with a bit of foam strip which is used to secure them into their designated space. This is really inadequate, considering that the foam will inevitably come into contact with water. Ask the builder to 'bed' the sink in an adhesive, preferably silicone, as this has some give built into it. The only slight drawback is that you can't paint over silicone.

- You will always get a certain amount of condensation under a sink and should therefore check that the ends of chipboard worktops are sealed, otherwise you could end up with rather a soggy mess where the work surface meets the sink area. Again, silicone spread with a finger will suffice.

- Floor-standing units should only be fitted *after* floor tiles or flagstones have been laid; otherwise your levels will be all wrong. Ditto washing machines and dishwashers.

Sanitary fittings

- Well-fitted baths, basins and loos should have a 'service isolating valve' (called a Balostop – Trade Mark), which allows you to isolate each appliance should there be a problem that needs investigating; if, for example, you wanted to change a tap washer, you could then do it without stopping the water supply to the rest of the house. Underneath a loo it is mandatory to have one.

- You should be able to gain access to waste pipes from basins and baths. In a perfect world you should have access to every straight length of pipe up to a bend, so that you can 'rod' it, should it become blocked with, for example, hair balls (quite common). Rarely do plumbers bother to do this, mainly because it requires co-operation with the carpenter, who has to fit the appropriate removable box skirting; but you should insist upon it, even if it is inconvenient for the plumber and carpenter to get their act together! After all, you are the one who will have the unpleasant task of unblocking the pipes.

- For the same reason, bathsides should ideally be removable, so that you can gain access to Balostops and drain fittings if necessary.

Decorating

This is usually the last part of any renovation job and the rules for checking quality of workmanship are fairly straightforward. The reason you need to be extra vigilant is that the builder may be impatient to get on with his next commission, may want to get his men off site as soon as possible and so rush the final details. Don't let him, otherwise you will end up with paint dribbles that for ever eye you accusingly as you try to watch television.

- The key to good decorating practice is in the preparation. Check that all timber is rubbed down well before painting or staining takes place.

- If any boards have been nailed or screwed down, make sure that the indentations are filled and then sanded before being painted.

- Watch to see that the painter doesn't start sanding down close to an area that has just been decorated. This is quite common when the job is being rushed and results in a horribly grainy surface where dust has stuck to fresh paint.

- The same goes for floorboards that are to be sanded and stained. The floor should be free of all dust before staining takes place. And floors should be stained *after* walls have been emulsioned.

- The correct way to paint directly on to plaster is to start with a 'miss' coat, i.e. a diluted version of the paint. Otherwise, the second coat will come off, because new plaster, being very porous, sucks all the water out of the paint, preventing a good bond. I bet you didn't know that!

- If you are having wallpaper put up, any new plaster underneath should be given a coat of paint first. Otherwise the plaster may react with chemicals in the adhesive paste and discolour the wallpaper.

- It is always a good sign to see at least one coat of emulsion going up before sockets, radiators and light fittings are secured. It makes it easier to paint the wall/ceiling in its entirety and gives a much more professional finish. Likewise radiators are easier to paint when free standing.

- Putting the boot on the other foot, you should expect plaster to crack in places. This is quite normal. The builder should minimise it, but none the less it will happen, probably within four weeks of turning the central heating on. A canny householder will provide for this by negotiating a six-month redecorating clause in the contract.

- A word about sealants. Plaster-based sealants, such as Polyfilla, should be used when you want to achieve a hard, solid finish which can then be sanded and painted over. But for sealing skirting boards to walls, or for any other job where you need to allow for a bit of movement, an acrylic filler is much more practical because it has a bit of 'give'; it is not waterproof but you can paint over it. For baths, sinks or basins, where you need both flexibility and waterproof qualities, choose a silicone sealer. Again, just make sure that the builder is paying attention to these final but important details; in a rush job he might just be tempted to charge around with a large tube of general purpose gunge.

THE TRICKS BUILDERS GET UP TO

Checking the builder's work is one safeguard, but there are a number of other little tricks they can get up to and of which you should be aware. I'm not for one moment suggesting that they are all on the fiddle, but you should be a little bit clued up. Equally, there are practices which may seem odd to you, but are really quite understandable when you become familiar with the nature of building work. Once again, it's a question of having enough knowledge to protect yourself and prevent unnecessary conflict with the builder.

Purchase of materials

A builder will almost always get a minimum 30 per cent trade discount when purchasing materials, but will not necessarily pass that saving on to you. You can accept this as:

- one of his perks;
- part of his profit margin;
- his way of funding the first four weeks of the job.

Or alternatively:

- ask if you can source the materials personally and take a chance on negotiating a discount;
- ask him to help you make the purchase and split the discount.

The DIY superstores have somewhat smashed the price cartel that used to operate among builders' merchants against Joe Public, so you may well get a good deal. But equally you must realise that if the 30 per cent really is part of the builder's profit margin and you take it away from him, he will simply raise the labour cost to compensate. So try to find out the basis of his quote before you act. A good builder will look for a living, not a killing.

Advance payments

Generally speaking, you should never pay a builder in advance. In a sense, he is running a business like anyone else, and should have the wherewithall to fund the first four weeks' work, especially since he gets preferential credit terms with suppliers. So don't fall for that one. However, there might be occasions when you want to use a small (but reputable) firm, maybe just one person, who can't fund the outlay. Rather than paying him in advance, offer to set up an account in your own name at the builder's merchants. You then buy the materials together and once again, he can help you get a trade discount.

Pilfering

It is common for builders to allow 10–15 per cent within their budget for losses due to pilfering. This either happens because opportunists take their pick during the night or because the builder is a bad boss and his workmen supplement their income with a few roof tiles. Either way, you are paying for it. One answer is to agree at the outset to provide the builder with a lockable site container; this can cost as little as £10 per week (1995 prices) and will enable you to lock up your materials and protect them. If things subsequently disappear, you know that it can only be the builder or his men!

Moving materials off site

This is a harder one to spot. Some builders will charge the client for materials and then keep a few bits back for another job, charging that client for the same items. While you can be watchful and check that the three drain covers you paid for are being used, it is harder to keep track of every bag of cement, roll of wire and bag of nails. The lock-up container is again the best solution, but I think you have to accept that one or two items might well go for a walk. However, you do have some protection if you have agreed a firm price for the job, as anything that disappears will have to be replaced at the builder's own expense.

Moving men off site

This is an interesting one. The official line is that your builder should, to use technical jargon, 'proceed regularly and diligently', but in the real world there will almost inevitably be some redeployment of manpower. At first sight it seems like a case of the builder losing interest towards the end of a job and sending parts of his team off to other sites. Again, if you only pay against work completed, you have some protection, even if it is irritating. But try also to look at it from the builder's point of view. Very few builders know when or where the next job is coming from and are subsequently loathe to turn anything down, even if it conflicts with an existing project. So they spend a lot of their time juggling men between sites, if only to maintain a presence and retain both jobs. This isn't your problem, I know, but the builder cannot even allow for this in his estimate, because a less scrupulous firm will simply promise to do the job in less time and scoop the contract. It really is dog eat dog out there. All you can do is let the builder know from day one that you are aware of this possibility, and make a time allowance for this in the contract. It is much better all round if the builder can be honest about this from day one.

GETTING THE BEST OUT OF YOUR BUILDER

It is really just common sense to help your builder whenever possible. Not only will he get the job done faster, but you will get the quality and service expected and stay on good terms into the bargain. Make sure that you agree on the following before work starts:

- Which rooms are to be cleared, by whom and by when.

- Where the builder can store equipment on site, and how/when he can gain access to it.

- Use of electricity, i.e. who is going to provide power for tools and equipment.

- Exactly when the builder can work in the house (remember your neighbours) and the order in which things are to be done, so that you know when the mess and inconvenience are likely to be at their greatest.

- Access through the house, so that you can protect carpets, etc., from dirty boots.

- Where the builder and his men can take a break, make tea, relax, park, so that they have some basic facilities and don't waste precious time going elsewhere for them.

- Whether or not they are allowed to play a radio, partly for your sake but equally for your neighbours'.

- Which bathroom facilities they can use. You may feel strongly about this and not want them using yours. If so, tell the builder well in advance of the job so that he can make alternative arrangements.

- How much access they have to the telephone. Making calls in relation to the job is fine, but you want to draw the line at the builder running his business from your 'phone. Agree a basis on which it can be used.

- Where they can shelter in case of bad weather. This obviously relates to work outside, but you will need to agree whether they can shelter in the garage/shed/house, etc.

- Your daily routine, if you are at home during the day, so that you interfere with each other as little as possible.

So, you've kept your beady little eye on the builder and everything has gone just perfectly – and was that a white rabbit I saw disappearing down the corridor? Well, I hope for your sake that your renovation works do go exactly to plan, but if they don't, here's what you do . . .

CHAPTER EIGHT

Satisfaction Guaranteed

'If anything can go wrong, it will, and at the most inopportune time' (*Murphy's Law*)

By far the greatest number of complaints received by Trading Standards Offices relate to home improvements. So when a job has been completed to your satisfaction you should just say a silent prayer of thanks and pay up. Unfortunately though, Murphy's Law and the business of renovating property are such that even with the most careful planning and execution you are likely to encounter one or two problems along the way. The bad news is that they will be difficult, if not impossible, to gauge in advance – dodgy workmanship is only apparent after it has been completed and faulty goods normally have to be used before the fault shows itself. The good news is that you have well-defined statutory rights which should be applied to the full. Never let anyone – builder, shop or manufacturer – fob you off if their goods or services have proved unsatisfactory. So pay attention to the following.

WHEN AND HOW TO PAY

The short answer is that you pay only when the work has been completed to your full satisfaction, i.e. that it should be fit for its purpose, done in a workmanlike manner and with proper materials. Having said that, you should pay promptly once those criteria have been fulfilled. Don't try to dodge or delay paying as it simply isn't fair and you may end up with a bucket of quick-setting cement down your drains! Your method of payment should be clearly laid out in your agreement with the builder (see Chapter Three) but if you are in any doubt as to how and when to pay, do as the professionals do: agree on weekly or monthly evaluations whereby you assess what the builder has done against the specification. It follows that under this system he has to explain and justify very clearly anything that has been done which differs from the original agreement.

You then come up with a gross valuation of what has been done (following the price given in the spec) and pay that amount, minus a 5 – 10 per cent retention for defective work. If you have agreed with the builder that he takes the initiative and invoices you in instalments, make sure that the amounts he invoices tie in with what was quoted on the specification; if you are in any doubt, keep a piece of paper with the works itemised down the left hand side of the page, the price quoted next to each one and then the amounts invoiced (as they come in) in columns on the right hand side. You will quickly see if you are paying more (or less!) than the agreed amount.

Your payments should always be in arrears, with the possible exception of:

- kitchen and bathroom fittings, which are often paid for in advance.

- any materials that you have agreed to pay for as you go along. Smaller builders may ask for payment for materials once on site and that is something you will have to decide on for yourself.

Towards the end of the job you should also draw up a final 'snag list', i.e. a list of all the little things which need minor adjustment, such as dripping taps, filling holes in wood, readjustment of the central heating system, etc. When this list has been attended to you should release approximately half the retention money, i.e. 2.5 – 5 per cent, and hold back the rest for the defects period, normally six months. Only ever pay out against an invoice and get it signed/receipted. Payment by cheque is more easily traceable than by cash. And lastly, never let a builder win the psychological battle of leaving the job unfinished but paid for because you have had enough and want some peace and quiet!

YOUR CONSUMER RIGHTS

It's nice to know that you are not totally alone in the world. Big Brother is not only watching you but also protecting you in law with certain 'statutory rights'. These apply regardless of any written or verbal contract you may have with a builder/other professional or supplier, extend to both goods and services and, in brief, are covered by:

The Sale of Goods Act 1979

This states (among other things) that goods bought from a trader must:

- fit the description given them;
- be of merchantable quality and last a reasonable length of time;
- be fit for their purpose.

The Supply of Goods and Services Act 1982

This applies only in England, Wales and N. Ireland, and details the standard of service you are entitled to, the quality of materials, price and timescale, and states that:

- anyone providing a service, e.g. building work, must do so with reasonable care and skill, within a reasonable time (where no time limit has been fixed) and at a reasonable charge (if no price has been fixed in advance).
- any goods supplied as part of a service, e.g. bathroom fittings, must be fit for their normal purpose, fit for any special purpose you have stipulated to the supplier and 'as described' by the supplier.

The Consumer Protection Act 1987

This is known as the (N.I.) Order 1987 in Northern Ireland. It states that:

- the manufacturer is liable if his product is defective and causes either personal injury or damage to property over £275;
- all goods must comply with general safety requirements;
- traders must follow certain guidelines when quoting for goods and services.

The Consumer Arbitration Agreements Act 1988

This states that for disputed sums under £1000 (£750 in Scotland), consumers have the right to choose between court action and arbitration, regardless of clauses in contracts which state that the matter has to be decided by arbitration.

Unfair Contract Terms Act 1977

This renders invalid any contract clause or condition which seeks (unreasonably) to restrict the rights of the purchaser with regard to compensation, etc. These rights are protected under the Sale of Goods Act and can never be taken away.

The Trade Descriptions Act 1968

You are also indirectly protected by criminal law. Under this Act it is an offence to make false statements about work done or materials used, either verbally or in writing, and transgressions can be prosecuted by the Trading Standards Department.

The following points are also worth noting. Some apply to services provided, others to goods you may have bought, for example, on behalf of the builder. If he buys them on your behalf but with his own money, your redress lies with him and in turn, his with the supplier. But for any goods or services you buy directly with your own money, your own statutory rights come into play.

Goods

- If you are unhappy with an item, return it to the point of purchase as soon as possible, or telephone to explain the problem.

- If your problem is not resolved to your satisfaction, follow up with a letter, preferably to a named individual. Always keep a copy, as well as any other supporting information, e.g. receipts, background information, photographic evidence, etc.

- You can request a refund on the grounds that you 'reject' the goods, i.e. refuse to accept them, although this must be done as quickly as possible, otherwise you might be deemed to have 'accepted' the goods

157

by keeping them for a 'reasonable' length of time. Only settle for a replacement or repair if that is what you really want.

- Be careful about signing 'acceptance' notes (as opposed to delivery notes) when items are delivered to you, as this may affect your right to a refund.

- Always check whether or not your purchase is under guarantee, as this can help you if your statutory rights don't apply for some reason (although only in Scotland is a manufacturer's guarantee legally enforceable). This can be particularly useful if you only discover the fault after using the goods for a while.

- Unless you are making a claim under a guarantee, it is the seller's responsibility to compensate you for defective goods, not the manufacturer's, so don't be fobbed off. This right also applies to faulty materials used in work done by your builder.

- Your rights apply even if you don't still have a receipt, but you may need some proof of purchase, e.g. a credit card voucher.

- You can sometimes claim compensation if you suffer loss as a result of faulty goods, e.g. damage to carpets from a faulty radiator.

- You are not legally obliged to return faulty goods at your expense.

Services

- Remember that you can claim compensation for breach of contract or negligence for up to six years (five in Scotland) and three years in the case of personal injury.

- The Latent Damage Act 1986 can protect you against faulty building or design work for up to 15 years after the work was done.

- Be careful about signing 'acceptance notes' for work completed, especially if you have not had a chance fully to inspect it.

- You can also claim compensation if the work done by, for example, a builder causes losses to your property you would not otherwise have incurred, e.g. if he drops paint on your carpet, you are entitled to some or all of the cost of cleaning or replacing that carpet.

- Remember that your builder is responsible for the work done by his subcontractors, so don't try and let him tell you otherwise.

- Lastly, a general point that applies to both services and goods. If you have paid by credit card or via a finance company loan arranged by the building firm, and the amount was between £100 and £30,000 (under £15,000 for a loan), the finance or credit card company are 'jointly liable' with the firm for any breach of contract or misrepresentation. This cover comes under the Consumer Credit Act 1974 and can be especially useful if the firm has gone bust, as you may still be able to claim compensation.

GUARANTEES

Guarantees are really an added protection for goods or services purchased. Your rights under a guarantee are in addition to your statutory rights and cannot limit the latter in any way. Not every product or service will automatically come with a free guarantee (there is no legal obligation to offer one) but the following are fairly standard:

1. Workmanship, e.g. plumbing and electrics – normally comes with at least a twelve-month guarantee, but watch out for the caveats; an electrician won't take responsibility for a piece of wiring if someone else has subsequently driven a nail through it. You will, of course, bypass all this if you are dealing directly with a builder, who will be responsible for all the work done under him.

2. Materials, e.g. roof tiles – some roof tiles come with a manufacturer's hundred-year guarantee (!) but generally speaking the length of time depends on the nature of the item and more important, how it has been handled. Most manufacturers produce manuals which go into great detail as to exactly how the product should be fitted. If it is not done according to the instructions or if the product is not used for the purpose for which it was intended, the manufacturer can challenge a claim. If possible, it is always a good idea to write off for the manual and also ask the builder to confirm in writing that an item has been fitted in accordance with the manufacturer's instructions, thus confirming that the guarantee on the product is valid. If nothing else you could use the manual to check up (discreetly!) on the builder while work is in progress.

3. Fittings, e.g. windows, doors, kitchens, bathrooms – again, the

length of time the product is under guarantee can vary, typically, from 5 to 30 years, and the small print may make a distinction depending upon whether or not the manufacturer has been allowed to install his own product. Again, always ask for and hang on to a copy of the terms.

4. Treatments, e.g. against rot or damp – very often the guarantee is for 30 years or more. If you do seem to have problems after the treatment has taken place, don't be palmed off by someone assuring you that the treatment was carried out. That isn't the point – you have paid for the treatment to have an effect, not just to know that the powder/paste, etc., has been applied in the right place. It costs companies money to keep coming out to put things right, and they will always try to avoid it if possible.

Here are some general points to look out for:

1. You can take over a guarantee from a previous owner, e.g. for a damp-proof course, but do contact the company to make sure that:

   ■ they are still trading;
   ■ the guarantee is transferable (you may have to pay a fee);
   ■ the guarantee is still valid; I know of someone who took over a damp-proof course guarantee only to be told that it had been invalidated by the previous owner rendering over the dpc. The fact that it could be chipped away was irrelevant – the company seized on the opportunity to annul the guarantee.

2. The length of time in a guarantee often sounds very generous, but won't mean a thing if the supplier goes bust. Ideally, the guarantee should also be backed up by insurance (see Chapter Three), but this isn't very common. Still, it is something to ask about.

WHAT TO DO WHEN THINGS GO WRONG

If you have a complaint against your builder (see Chapter Two for complaints against other professionals), there are several possible courses of action:

Negotiation

If something is not to your satisfaction, tell the builder straightaway. Don't leave it until the end of the job, as he might view this just as a ruse to get a reduction on the bill. Most builders will be happy to remedy problems as they go along, and see this as just another part of the job. But if they have already finished the contract, make it clear that you are going to withhold a (reasonable) part of the final payment until this work is done, over and above the defects provision. And do get them to commit themselves to a time. Don't accept some vague promise about turning up 'sometime soon' to put things right.

As soon as something goes wrong, start keeping records of exactly what is said and done. If you have telephoned the contractor, make a note of the date and time of your call, whom you spoke to and what was discussed. Follow this up in writing and send your correspondence by recorded delivery whenever possible. Always keep copies of any letters you send and never let go of original documents such as receipts or guarantees. Sending photocopies is perfectly acceptable.

Appealing to their association

I hope you have used someone who is a member of either the FMB, the BEC, or the GMC. As such, they have agreed to abide by a code of conduct and the association can put considerable moral pressure on them to handle your complaint (note that these codes of practice are not legally binding). It is of course at times like these that you would rejoice in having subscribed to the FMB guarantee scheme referred to on p. 49 (what do you mean, you didn't?) although obviously it is only relevant for FMB members.

Arbitration

If your trader is a member of an association, there may be an arbitration scheme available for settling disputes. Even if he isn't, you can arrange arbitration independently. Either way, both sides have to agree to participate. The procedure is simple and involves the following:

- both you and the builder sign an 'application for arbitration', which is sent to the association administering the scheme together with a registration fee.
- you, i.e. the claimant, complete a 'statement of claim' and return this,

together with all supporting documentation and a registration fee, to the relevant association.

- the trader submits similar information to support his case. ¯
- the arbitrator reads the documentation and possibly makes site visits, etc. He will be an expert in the area concerned and may be a member of the Chartered Institute of Arbitrators (Arbiters in Scotland). His decision is binding. Both parties are informed in writing as to the outcome.

If you have opted for independent arbitration and lose the case, you will have to bear the costs of the arbitrator. Otherwise, the trade association will normally foot the bill. You can use this procedure instead of, but not as well as, going to court. NB. Under the Consumer Arbitration Agreements Act 1988, a clause in a contract which says that you have to go to arbitration cannot bind you so long as the value of your dispute is less than or equal to the small claims limit.

Enlisting outside help

Your local Trading Standards (or Consumer Protection) Department, Citizens Advice Bureau or Consumer Advice Centre can all be extremely helpful. You will first need to help them by supplying as much background paperwork as possible. Then they can contact the builder on your behalf, especially if he is local and known to them. If relevant, they can prosecute under the Trade Descriptions Act and Sale of Goods and Services Act. Most builders will attempt to sort out your complaint before this happens.

Going to court

This should be viewed as a last resort and only after a 'letter before action', which gives the builder a final chance to settle the matter. It will, of course, be fruitless if your builder has gone bankrupt. So check his position before getting involved in form-filling and fees. There are two alternatives:

1. The County Court

This is likely to be your first port of call. It can determine claims of up to £50,000, for things such as bad workmanship, faulty goods and goods not supplied. In Scotland the equivalent is the Sheriff Court. Claims are divided into two kinds: those under £1000 and those over.

– Those under £1000 (at the time of writing, but likely to be increased to £2500). Amounts under £1000 (£750 in Scotland) are called *small claims* and these days the procedure has been considerably simplified to help people settle their differences with minimum fuss and expense. You complete a County Court Summons form N1. The form requests basic details of your claim and is straightforward to fill in. If you are making a claim against more than one person you will need a form for each one of them. Send it to your local county court with the appropriate fee (which varies from £10 upwards). They will issue a receipt for your fee and give you a case reference number. You then wait for confirmation (called a 'notice of issue') from the court that the defendant has received the summons. The defendant then has 14 days to return the reply form with either payment, part payment, a counter claim or explanation as to why they don't intend to pay.

If the defendant admits the claim he will make an offer to pay via form N9A, which the court will then help you to enforce by sending the defendant a form stating how much to pay, when to pay it and where to send payment. If he doesn't bother to reply, the court will automatically enter 'judgment by default' (using form N30) and send the defendant notice of how he must pay. If the defendant decides to defend all or part of the claim, he will complete form N9B; if you accept this offer of part payment the court will send the defendant an order to pay you (this is called 'entering judgment on acceptance'). If you do not accept it you have to fill in part A of form N225A and send this to the court. The details of your case will then be passed to the district judge who will instigate one of the following:

- a 'preliminary appointment', whereby the judge decides that an initial meeting to see both you and the defendant is necessary. Form N18 is used to tell you when and where this appointment will take place. If there is no possibility of settling the dispute at this time, the judge will further consider how the case should be dealt with, namely . . .

- an 'arbitration hearing' (not to be confused with the arbitration mentioned above), whereby you sit in private with the judge who listens to both sides of the case and then makes a decision. If the judge chooses this option, you will be sent form N18A – notice of arbitration hearing – which will clarify exactly what information you have to prepare, the time, date and place of the hearing. Subsequent to the arbitration you will be sent details of the arbitrator's decision (called the 'award'), which will set out how much money has to be paid and to whom.

- a trial in open court, if your case is too complicated to be dealt with via a small claim. The main advantage of the small claims court is one of cost. If you win the case, you can request the court fee, expenses, loss of earnings of £29 and up to £112.50 reimbursement of experts' fees. But if you lose the case, expenses, loss of earnings and experts' fees can be awarded against you.

There is an excellent series of leaflets, available from local county courts, which explains small claims very clearly.

– Those claims over £1000. If the amount in dispute is over £1000 the procedure is slightly different. You begin by filling in the same summons form and waiting 14 days for a reply from the defendant. But if he wants to defend the claim it has to be heard before a district judge in open court. If the amount is over £5000, it is heard before a more senior 'circuit judge', again in open court. You can still represent yourself, but with larger amounts at stake, you may want a solicitor in your corner. If you lose, you might have to pay both sides' legal fees.

2. The High Court

If your claim is for more than £50,000 or if the county court deems it necessary on a point of law, you will have to go through the high court procedure. The 'point of law' could become relevant if there was a dispute over, for example, 'causation'; you might be arguing over subsidence, but the court would have to decide whether this was inherent in the property when you bought it or whether the builder caused it. Another example would be if you had a problem with a subcontractor but either didn't have a contract with the builder or had one which didn't stipulate where responsibility should lie. The high court option can get very expensive, especially as most people choose professional representation. The main advantage of the high court procedure is that there is provision for appeal if things don't go your way. But you really want to avoid this alternative if at all possible.

This is a somewhat sober note to end on, and I hope you won't have to take such drastic action.

Conclusion

As you have no doubt realised by now, the key to successful property renovation is planning and organisation. Planning, so that you know what you want and can afford, whose help you might need, and that all the appropriate official permissions and utility requirements are in place. Then organising yourself, the builder and your paperwork so that the renovation work goes as smoothly as possible. You can't hope to control everything, and finding a good builder is a *sine qua non* of success, but solid preparation counts for a lot, and can save you a great deal of money and anguish. Above all, allow yourself plenty of time, because building works, and especially renovations, almost always take longer than expected – both in the preparation stage and when they are in progress. Figure 23 is a summary of the total renovation process, and it places particular emphasis on the time you should allocate to preparation before works begin.

Last, and if at all possible, try to retain a sense of humour throughout the proceedings! By all means educate yourself to be able to follow and assess what the builder is doing, but also remember that you will get a lot more out of him through reasoned discussion and reasonable requests than through veiled threats. Your dream home is but a renovation away. I wish you many happy hours among the dust and debris. Good luck – oh, and do try not to fall through the ceiling.

Figure 23. Chart of Total Renovation Process

BEFORE START DATE

3 months	2 months	1 months	During works	After works
1. Develop spec • have structural survey • establish objectives • establish budget 2. Check if work affects party wall agreements 3. Check deeds of the property - especially if it is leasehold 4. Check with landlord if applicable 5. Choose builder 6. Decide if other professional help needed 7. Make planning and building regulations applications 8. Order long lead time items eg. units for kitchens	1. Organise utility requirements 2. Organise any necessary accommodation	1. Draw up room plans 2. Familiarise yourself with the order of renovation works	1. Monitor progress at site meetings and confirm everything in writing 2. Agree terms on any unforeseen works 3. Anticipate possible delays and have alternative jobs lined up 4. Check quality of work in progress 5. Arrange necessary site inspections for building regulations 6. Deliver certificate of inspection to electricity board 7. Make any staged payments against completed works 8. Purchase materials (if agreed with builder)	1. Go through the `snag' list 2. Make final payments 3. Hold back the retention money 4. Have the builder carry out any necessary repairs 5. Complete paperwork. File: • guarantees • receipts • invoices • general correspondence

Maintenance Checklist

You've come this far, so capitalise on all the hard work by keeping your property in tip-top condition with regular checks. The time involved is minimal and so too will be the expense, but only if you know what to look for. The best time to do this is in the spring, the traditional time for painting and decorating, and late autumn, when exterior repairs can be put right before bad weather prevents work and does yet more damage. Your checklist should include:

Roof
Don't clamber round on roofs – it's dangerous. Try to identify the problem from within the loft first; after all, the enemy is water and only when you find it inside the house. So look for signs of water penetration. Outside you can use binoculars to:

- Check flat roofs for cracked or worn patches of felt and loose flashing.
- Check tile roofs for damaged or missing tiles.
- Check eaves, verges and ridges – the most common areas for wear and tear.

Chimneys
- Look to make sure that mortar, pointing and lead flashing are all in place.
- If the chimney is in use, have it swept.
- If the chimney is no longer in use, check that it is ventilated, to prevent damp in the chimney breast.

Gutters and downpipes
- Best to check on a rainy day, when the equipment is being used.
- All water should flow away smoothly and leaves/debris be removed.
- Check for standing water near the house.
- In metal gutters look for leaking joints and rust holes.
- In plastic gutters check for worn rubber seals.
- Make sure that all gutter supports are adequate.

Drains
- Lift inspection chamber lids and look for blockages.
- Make sure that solids haven't been washed up on to the benching.

Walls
- Watch out for damp caused by defective guttering.
- Check brickwork for loose mortar joints and splitting.
- Check render for hairline cracks and loose areas.
- Check paintwork for peeling.

Damp-proof course
- Outside the property, check that debris and soil is not stacked up against the wall. If it is, it should be at least 150 mm (6 inches) below the damp-proof course level.

Condensation
- Not to be confused with damp. Check for wet window sills on a dry day (as opposed to damp caused by wet weather or a leak) and improve ventilation, especially in bathrooms and kitchens.

Airbricks
- Make sure that airbricks are kept clear. Garden debris can pile up and block them, especially if plants are grown against the wall.

Windows and doors
- Check window frames externally where they meet the wall; driving rain can penetrate any gap in the mastic and cause damp.
- Check that putty is sound.
- Check sills for rot.
- Check for draughts – these can be created by movement in wooden frames.
- Check the security of your window fasteners and locks.

Decorating
- Check that outside paint is sound; algae can form on north-facing walls.
- Peeling wallpaper/paint or salt deposits from bricks (efflorescence) can signify damp, the source of which may be some way from the damp patch itself.

Electricity
- Look for broken switches or sockets or brown heat marks around them.

Plumbing
- Check radiator valves, pipe joints, tap washers and ball-valves for leaks.
- Check that your tank is free from debris and blocked overflows.

Woodworm
- Look for the tell-tale pinhead holes in the surface of wood, especially untreated floorboards, window sills, wooden lintels, ceiling beams and the underside of stairs. A pile of dust around the hole indicates that the worm is active.

Rot
- Wet rot: check any areas of wood which are exposed to damp, e.g. window sills. Prod with a screwdriver if necessary.
- Dry rot: less obvious than wet rot but identifiable by its musty smell and cotton-wool-like appearance. Thrives in unventilated places such as cellars, under floors and stairs.

Insulation
Check that loft insulation is in place and in good condition. (Mice love to nest in it!)
- Check that pipes and tanks are lagged properly.

Heating appliances
- Have a regular service for all gas appliances – British Gas are excellent in this respect.
- Similarly, have coal and oil fires checked over once a year.

Glossary of Terms

AFL   Above floor level.

Aggregate   A mixture of sand and stone, generally used for cement and water to mix concrete.

Air brick   A brick with holes in, used for ventilation, usually below suspended floors.

Angle bead   A protective strip, used on external corners which are subsequently rendered or plastered.

Architrave   The trimming around a door lining, usually wood.

Arris   A piece of wood, triangular in section, used to pack space between two other pieces of wood.

Backfill   Soil or aggregate used to fill trench holes, e.g. footings.

Barge board   Gable end trim to conceal roof timbers.

Battens   The pieces of timber on which roof tiles are laid.

Beading   A small strip of timber used as a trim, e.g. round a door frame.

Bonding   A kind of plaster, used to fill holes in plasterboard.

Building regs   Statutory instruments issued by the government describing and requiring certain standards of building.

Carcassing   Cheap timber, normally used for partitions, etc.

Casement   The part of a window on hinges which opens and shuts, as opposed to the frame, which is the surround in which it hangs.

Cavity wall   A wall which has an inner and outer skin and cavity in between.

Cess pool   A large tank for collecting foul waste. It does not attempt to treat the waste. Only used where a septic tank or mains drainage is not practicable.

Chase   A groove in a wall used as a channel for electrical wiring and plumbing.

Cladding   A board or panel product used to cover portions of a building.

Corbel   A projection of stone or timber jutting out from a wall to support weight. Can also be decorative.

Coving   Plaster moulding placed between the junction of wall and ceiling.

Defects period   The length of time within which any defect is the responsibility of the builder to put right – normally included in the terms of contract.

170

Doorset Everything you need to install a door – the door lining, door itself and furniture (i.e. handle, lock, kickplate, etc.).

Downpipe A pipe which hangs vertically, internally or externally, and carries waste and rainwater from a building.

DPC A piece of water-impermeable membrane which sits between two structures to isolate wet parts from dry parts. It can also be a chemical treatment.

Dry rot A fungal infestation affecting masonry and timber. Pernicious stuff!

Earth Should refer to an electrical earth, not the brown muddy stuff!

Eaves The horizontal line at the bottom of a roof pitch.

Efflorescence Crystals of salt that grow on walls which are damp or drying out.

Estimate A builder's best guess at the cost of a job – a figure never known actually to go down!

Fair faced A concrete block which is clean, smooth and doesn't have to be rendered.

Fascia A piece of wood which runs horizontally below the eave and to which guttering is attached.

Felt Can be any of several types: roofing felt – the second line of defence for waterproofing, which lies over the rafters but under the battens; felt underlay for carpets; felt for lagging pipes.

First fix Where a trade, e.g. plumbing/electrics, logically fits into two stages, the 'first fix' refers to all the work which takes place before plastering.

Flashing Lead or tape used to seal the place where a roof meets a vertical wall or abutment, e.g. on a parapet wall or around chimneys.

Flaunching The cement finishing around a chimney.

Flux A wetting agent used when soldering.

FOC Free Of Charge. You probably won't come across this one very often . . .

Footings Concrete cast in trenches which forms the basis of foundation works.

Gable A piece of wall underneath a ridge.

Grouting The cement between tiles.

Gully A drain.

Hardboard A man-made board comprised of wood fibres and resin glues compressed during manufacture to form a dense board – not water resistant.

Hardcore Lumps of stone and rubble placed under a concrete slab.

Hardwood Timber from deciduous or evergreen trees (other than pine).

Header A strong member (timber or steel) used to support other structural members (joists or rafters).

Herringbone strut Two pieces of timber, crossed in an X shape, and placed between floor or ceiling joists to brace the joist and keep it upright.

Infill Material used to fill a hole, e.g. hardcore.

Insulating blocks Lightweight concrete blocks with improved insulating capability – softer and easier to drill into than standard concrete blocks.

Jamb i.e. of a door; the part of a door frame against which a door sits.

Joist A strong timber which holds up floors and ceilings.

Lintel A structural member (steel, concrete or wood) which supports a wall over an opening, e.g. a door or window.

Loadbearing wall   A wall which supports another wall, floor, roof or any other part of the structure which imposes a load.

Mains   A service coming into the property from outside, e.g. gas, electricity, water.

Miss coat   Diluted emulsion paint applied to fresh plaster to ensure good adhesion of subsequent coats of paint.

Mitre   A corner joint formed by two pieces of timber meeting. Formed by cutting bevels of equal angles at the ends of each piece.

Mortar   A mixture of sand, cement and plasticiser.

Mortice   A type of timber joint or a lock.

Newel   Staircase component supporting the handrails, also called a newel post.

Noggin   A short piece of timber used as bracing between studs, rafters or joists.

Pantile   A wavy roof tile, of clay or concrete.

PC   Used in specifications, meaning Prime Cost, i.e. the cost of buying a certain item as distinct from the cost of installing it.

Perpends   The vertical bit of mortar between two bricks (the horizontal bit is a 'bed').

Pitch   The slope of a roof, measured in degrees; *or* a tarry bitumen substance used as a sealant on flat roofs; *or* the angle of a staircase.

Planning permission   The process of obtaining consent from the local authority to alter or erect buildings.

Plasterboard   Gypsum plaster sandwiched between two pieces of strong paper.

Pointing   Mortar applied between bricks or stone as weather proofing.

Poppers   Small pieces of plaster, normally covering a nail or screw in a ceiling or wall, which are worked loose because the nail or screw is standing proud.

Purlins   Horizontal beams or strong pieces of wood used for supporting rafters.

Quilt   Normally a measure of fibreglass or rockwool used as loft insulation.

Quoin   Piece of stone set into the corner of a wall, giving strength to the structure.

Rafter   A structural timber spanning from the eave to the ridge of a roof and supporting the tiles.

Rebate   A section of timber removed to allow something to fit, e.g. the bottom of a door rebated over a weather strip.

Rendering   A coat of sand and cement applied to a wall, internally or externally.

Retention   Funds held back by the client as an insurance against repair.

Reveal   A bit of wall returning into a doorframe.

Ridge   The horizontal line at the top of a pitched roof.

RSJ   *aka* 'Rolled Steel Joist', used as a beam or lintel to support heavy loads.

Sash window   A particular design whereby the window opens by virtue of its two components sliding up and down across each other.

Satisfaction note   A letter/note from a client to a builder confirming that the work carried out by the latter is acceptable.

Screed   Coarse sand/cement mix applied as top coat over concrete to form a floor.

Second fix   *See First fix*; the second stage of e.g. plumbing or electrics, which takes place after plastering.

Septic tank   A large underground tank which collects foul waste from a building, processes it biologically and subsequently disperses it via a soakaway.

Sets   Pairs of walls, usually opposite, which are plastered at the same time.

Sewer   A large drain maintained by the local authority, serving several properties.

Shuttering   Or framework; a temporary or permanent structure erected to contain concrete while it sets.

Size   A chemical treatment applied to walls to prevent efflorescence or staining.

Skimming   The application of plaster to substrate.

Sleeper wall   A piece of wall no less than 15 cm (6 inches) high, which is used to support the floor joists underneath the ground floor floor.

Snots   Unwanted bits of plaster left on walls or superfluous mortar left between cavity walls (slang term).

Soffit   The piece of timber or plywood positioned under the barge board or fascia and at right angles to the wall, designed to seal the gap between the fascia/barge board and wall and to prevent birds or insects getting in.

Soil pipe   A large pipe for carrying foul waste from a sanitary appliance to a drain.

Solder   An alloy of lead and tin, used to join pipes.

Spalling   Breaking the edge or face of a brick or piece of concrete, often caused by expansion forces, e.g. rusting reinforcement rods, water freezing in cracks, or holes being drilled too close to the edge of concrete slabs.

Specification   A definitive document detailing works required (words or diagrams).

Stretcher   A brick laid horizontally, so that you can see the full length of its face.

String   The part of a staircase between the newels. Supports the treads and rises.

Stucco   A form of textured plastering or rendering.

Stud   A vertical timber, i.e. running from floor to ceiling.

Stud partition   Used to divide room space within a house and made up of studs clad with plasterboard and skimmed.

Substrate   The material on which you normally skim, i.e. plasterboard or render.

Sulphates   Chemical salts, e.g. iron or copper sulphate, which if present in the ground may attack and degrade concrete over a period of time; if present, a sulphate resisting cement must be used.

Trussed rafter   Or roof truss; a pre-fabricated (normally triangular) structure comprising rafters, ceiling joists and braces, all joined together using gang nail plates.

Vapour barrier   A water-impermeable membrane, located in a building in such a position as to prevent moisture passing from one side to the other, e.g. a polythene sheet put behind ceiling plasterboard to prevent moisture entering the roof void.

Waste pipe   A small-bore pipe, normally 40 or 35 mm ($1\frac{1}{2}$ or $1\frac{1}{4}$ inches), connecting a sink or basin to a drain.

Weather board   Timber used as cladding on the outside of a building, normally horizontal and nailed to vertical battens.

Wet rot   Decomposing wood due to continual exposure to water (quite distinct from dry rot).

Wet trades   Any plastering or rendering, both of which require lots of water.

Winder   A tread in a staircase which moves round a corner.

Resources

Organisations representing professionals

The following organisations represent professionals who work in the building and renovation industry. All will give lists of their members and details of their qualifications for membership upon request.

Architects' and Surveyors' Institute, 15 St Mary Street, Chippenham, Wiltshire SN15 3WD   Tel 01249 444505

Architects' Registration Council of the United Kingdom, 73 Hallam Street, London W1N 6EE   Tel 0171 580 5861 Fax 0171 436 5269

Association of Building Engineers, Jubilee House, Billingbrook Road, Weston Favell, Northamptonshire, NN3 8NW   Tel 01604 404121 Fax 01604 784220

Association of Consultant Architects, Buchanans Wharf, Redcliff Backs, Bristol BS1 6HT   Tel 0117 929 3379 Fax 0117 925 6008

Association of Consulting Engineers, Alliance House, Caxton Street, London SW1H 0QL   Tel 0171 222 6557

Association of Project Managers, 85 Oxford Road, High Wycombe, Bucks HP11 2DX   Tel 01494 440090 Fax 01494 528937

British Institute of Architectural Technologists, 397 City Road, London EC1V 1NE   Tel 0171 278 2206 Fax 0171 837 3194

British Woodworking Federation, 82 New Cavendish Street, London W1M 8AD   Tel 0171 580 5588

Builders' Merchants Federation, 15 Soho Square, London W1V 5FB Tel 0171 439 1753

Building Employers' Confederation, 82 New Cavendish Street, London W1M 8AD   Tel 0171 580 5588

174

Chartered Institution of Building Services Engineers, Delta House, 222 Balham High Road, London SW12 9BS   Tel 0181 675 5211

Carvers and Gilders, 9 Charterhouse Works, Eltringham Street, London SW18 1TD   Tel 0181 870 7047

Electrical Contractors' Association, ESCA House, 34 Palace Court, Bayswater, London W2 4HY   Tel 0171 229 1266 Fax 0171 221 7344

Electrical Contractors' Association of Scotland, Bush House, Bush Estate, Midlothian EH26 0SB   Tel 0131 445 5577

Federation of Plastering & Drywall Contractors, 18 Mansfield Street, London W1M 9FG   Tel 0171 580 5404 Fax 0171 636 5984

Federation of Master Builders, Gordon Fisher House, 14/15 Great James Street, London WC1N 3DP   Tel 0171 242 7583 Fax 0171 404 0296

Guild of Incorporated Surveyors, 1 Alexandra Street, Queens Road, Oldham OL8 2AU   Tel 0161 627 2389

Guild of Master Craftsmen, Castle Place, 166 High Street, Lewes, East Sussex BN7 1XU   Tel 01273 478449 Fax 01273 478606

Heating and Ventilation Contractors' Association, ESCA House, 34 Palace Court, Bayswater, London W2 4JG   Tel 0171 229 2488

Incorporated Society of Valuers and Auctioneers, 3 Cadogan Gate, London SW1X 0AS   Tel 0171 235 2282 Fax 0171 235 4390

Institute of Clerks of Works, 41 The Mall, Ealing, London W5 3TJ Tel 0181 579 2917/8 Fax 0181 579 0554

Institute of Electrical Engineers, Savoy Place, London WC2R 0BL Tel 0171 240 1871

Institute of Gas Engineers, 21 Portland Place, London W1N 3AF Tel 0171 636 6603

Institute of Plumbing, 64 Station Lane, Hornchurch, Essex RM12 6NB Tel 01708 472791

League of Professional Craftsmen, 10 Village Way, Raynes Lane, Pinner HA5 5AF   Tel 0181 866 6116

Master Locksmiths' Association, Unit 4–5, The Business Park, Woodford Halse, Daventry, Northamptonshire NN11 3PZ   Tel 01327 62255

National Association of Chimney Sweeps, St Mary's Chambers, Station Road, Stone, Staffordshire ST15 8JP   Tel 01785 811732

National Association of Loft Insulation Contractors, PO Box 12, Haslemere, Surrey GU27 3AH   Tel 01428 654011

National Association of Plumbing, Heating and Mechanical Services Contractors, Ensign House, Ensign Business Centre, Westwood Way, Coventry CV4 8JA   Tel 01203 470626 Fax 01203 470942

National Association of Scaffolding Contractors, 18 Mansfield Street, London W1M 9FG   Tel 0171 580 5404 Fax 0171 636 5984

National Federation of Painting and Decorating Contractors, 82 New Cavendish Street, London W1M 8AD   Tel 0171 580 5404 Fax 0171 636 5984

National Federation of Roofing Contractors Limited, 24 Weymouth Street, London W1N 3FA   Tel 0171 436 0387 Fax 0171 637 5215

National Inspection Council for Electrical Installation Contracting, 37 Albert Embankment, London SE1 7UJ   Tel 0171 582 7746

Royal Incorporation of Architects in Scotland, 15 Rutland Square, Edinburgh EH1 2BE   Tel 0131 229 7205

Royal Institute of British Architects, 66 Portland Place, London W1N 4AD Tel 0171 580 5533 RIBA Publications: 0171 251 0791

Royal Institution of Chartered Surveyors (Headquarters), 12 Great George Street, Parliament Square, Westminster, London SW1P 3AD Tel 0171 222 7000 Fax 0171 222 9430

Royal Institution of Chartered Surveyors in Scotland, 9 Manor Place, Edinburgh EH3 7DN   Tel 0131 225 7078

Royal Society of Ulster Architects, 2 Mount Charles, Belfast BT7 1NZ Tel 01232 323760

Scottish Building Employers' Federation, 13 Woodside Crescent, Glasgow G3 7UP   Tel 0141 332 7144

Scottish and Northern Ireland Plumbing Employers' Federation, 2 Walker Street, Edinburgh EH3 7LB   Tel 0131 225 2255

Society of Architects in Wales, 75a Llandennis Road, Rhydypennau, Cardiff CF2 6EE   Tel 01222 762215

Environmental and planning advisory/ regulatory bodies

Department of the Environment, 2 Marsham Street, London SW1P 3EB Tel 0171 276 0900

Department of the Environment Planning Inspectorate (Appeals), Tollgate House, Houlton Street, Bristol BS2 9DJ   Tel 0117 987 8000

Royal Town Planning Institute, 26 Portland Place, London W1N 4BE Tel 0171 636 9107

Secretary of State for Wales, Welsh Office, Crown Buildings, Cathays Park, Cardiff CF1 3NQ

Historic buildings and conservation

These associations have a wealth of knowledge on all aspects of renovating and maintaining old buildings.

Cadw/Welsh Historic Monuments, Brunel House, 2 Fitzalan Road, Cardiff CF2 1UY   Tel 01222 465511

English Heritage, Enquiry Point, Fortress House, 23 Savile Row, London W1X 1AB   Tel 0171 973 3000. North Region: 0171 973 3020. Midlands Region: 0171 973 3018. South Region: 0171 973 3008. London Region: 0171 973 3716. London Grants Branch based at Chesham House, 30 Warwick Street, London W1R 5RD

The Georgian Group, 37 Spital Square, London E1 6DY   Tel 0171 377 1722

Historic Scotland, Heritage Policy Group 3, 133 Longmore House, Salisbury Place, Edinburgh EH9 1SH   Tel 0131 662 1250

Northern Ireland Housing Executive, The Housing Centre, 2 Adelaide St, Belfast BT2 8PB   Tel 01232 317000

Upkeep (formerly the Building Conservation Trust), Apartment 39, Hampton Court Palace, East Molesey, Surrey KT8 9BS   Tel 0181 943 2277 Fax 0181 943 9552

The Victorian Society, 1 Priory Gardens, Bedford Park, London W4 1TT Tel 0181 994 1019

Society for the Protection of Ancient Buildings, 37 Spital Square, London E1 6DY   Tel 0171 377 1644 Fax 0171 247 5296

The building industry

The following associations represent the building industry.

Chartered Institute of Arbitrators, 24 Angel Gate, City Road, London EC1V 2RS   Tel 0171 837 4483

Chartered Institute of Building, Englemere, King's Ride, Ascot, Berkshire SL5 8BJ   Tel 01344 23355 Fax 01344 23467

Construction Industry Council, 26 Store Street, London WC1E 7BT Tel 0171 637 8692

Institute of Building Control, 21 High Street, Ewell, Epsom, Surrey KT17 1SB   Tel 0181 393 6860 Fax 0181 393 1083

Building materials

These associations represent the manufacturers of building materials and can give out lists of members as well as advice on where to find products.

Brick Development Association, Woodside House, Winkfield, Windsor, Berkshire SL4 2DX   Tel 01344 885651 Fax 01344 890129

Draught Proofing Advisory Association, PO Box 12, Haslemere, Surrey, GU27 3AH   Tel 01428 654011

Glass and Glazing Federation, 44-48 Borough High Street, London SE1 1XB   Tel 0171 403 7177 Fax 0171 357 7458

Stone Federation of Great Britain, 18 Mansfield Street, London W1M 9FG Tel 0171 580 5404 Fax 0171 636 5984

Timber and Brick Homes Information Council, Gable House, 40 High Street, Rickmansworth, Hertfordshire WD1 3ES   Tel 01923 778136

Timber Research and Development Association (TRADA), Stocking Lane, Hughenden Valley, High Wycombe, Bucks HP14 4ND   Tel 01494 563091

Insurance, security, health and safety advice

The following bodies will give out lists of their members.

Association of British Insurers, 51–55 Gresham Street, London EC2V 7HQ Tel 0171 600 3333

British Security Industry Association Ltd, Security House, Barbourne Road, Worcester WR1 1RS   Tel 01905 21464 Fax 01905 613625

Building Guarantee Scheme Ltd, 143 Malone Road, Belfast BT9 6SU Tel 01232 661717

Fire Protection Association, 140 Aldersgate Street, London EC1A 4HY Tel 0171 606 3757

Guarantee Protection Trust Ltd, 27 London Road, High Wycombe, Buckinghamshire HP11 1BW   Tel 01494 447049

Health and Safety Executive Information Centre, Broad Lane, Sheffield, S3 7HQ   Tel 0114 289 2345 Fax 0114 289 2333

Independent Warranty Association, 21 Albion Place, Northampton NN1 1UD   Tel 01604 604511

National Supervisory Council for Intruder Alarms, Queensgate House, 14 Cookham Road, Maidenhead, Berkshire SL6 8AJ   Tel 01628 37512

Fixtures and fittings

This association gives out useful information on choosing the right facilities for your bathroom. I found their 'design' advice particularly helpful.

British Bathroom Council, Federation House, Stoke-on-Trent, Staffordshire ST4 2RT   Tel 01782 747074 Fax 01782 747161

Heating, lighting and energy conservation

The following are all good sources of information.

British Coal (Head Office), Hobart House, Grosvenor Place, London SW1X 7AE   Tel 0171 201 4141

British Gas plc (Head Office), 326 High Holborn, London WC1V 7PT Tel 0171 242 0789

Corgi (The Council for Registered Gas Installers), 4 Elmwood, Chineham Business Park, Crockford Lane, Basingstoke, Hampshire, RG24 8WG Tel 01256 707060

Department of Energy/Efficiency, 2 Marsham Street, London SW1P 3EB Tel 0171 276 4975

Energy Action Grants Agency, PO Box 1NG, Newcastle upon Tyne NE99 1NG   Tel 01800   181667

Lighting Association, Stafford Park 7, Telford, Shropshire TF3 3BQ Tel 01952 290905 Fax 01952 290906

National Cavity Insulation Association, PO Box 12, Haslemere, Surrey GU27 3AH   Tel 01428 654011

National Energy Foundation, Rockingham Drive, Linford Wood, Milton Keynes MK14 6EG   Tel 01908 672787

Office of Electricity Regulation, Hagley House, 83–85 Hagley Road, Edgbaston, Birmingham B16 8QG   Tel 0121 456 2100

Office of Gas Supply, Stockley House, 130 Wilton Road, London SW1V 1LQ   Tel 0171 828 0898

Infestation and pest control

These associations represent infestation and pest control companies, and can give out lists of members and basic advice on what to look out for in your own home.

British Pest Control Association, 3 St James's Court, Friar Gate, Derby DE1 1ZU   Tel 01332 294288 Fax 01332 295904

British Wood Preserving and Damp-proofing Association, Building No. 6, The Office Village, 4 Romford Road, Stratford, London E15 4EA Tel 0181 519 2588 Fax 0181 519 3444

Quality control advice

These associations can give advice on which products conform to current safety and quality standards.

British Standards Institution, BSI Enquiries, Linford Wood, Milton Keynes, Bucks MK14 6LE   Tel 01908 226888

BSI Quality Assurance Certification and Assessment, Linford Wood, Milton Keynes MK14 6LL   Tel 01908 220908

Associations representing utilities

Office of Telecommunications, Export House, 50 Ludgate Hill, London EC4M 7JJ   Tel 0171 634 8700

Office of Water Services, Centre City Tower, 7 Hill Street, Birmingham B5 4UA   Tel 0121 625 1300

Financial representatives

All will give out lists of their members.

Building Societies Association/Council of Mortgage Lenders, 3 Savile Row, London W1X 1AF   Tel 0171 437 0655

Finance and Leasing Association, 18 Upper Grosvenor Street, London W1X 9PB   Tel 0171 491 2783

Consumer advice

Consumers' Association, 2 Marylebone Road, London NW1 4DF
Tel 0171 830 6000

National Association of Citizens Advice Bureaux, 115–123 Pentonville Road, London NW1 9LZ   Tel 0171 833 2181

Office of Fair Trading, Field House, 15–25 Bream's Buildings, London EC4A 1PR   Tel 0171 242 2858

Small Claims Court, Lord Chancellor's Department, Trevelyan House, 30 Great Peter Street, London SW1P 2BY   Tel 0171 210 3000

Additional sources of publications/contracts

The Building Centre, 26 Store Street, London WC1B 7BT
Tel 0171 637 1022 Fax 0171 580 9641. This has an unrivalled supply of free leaflets on thousands of building products, plus a Building Bookshop which stocks over 1000 titles, a number of building magazines and various contracts. There is a mail order service.

Joint Contracts Tribunal, RIBA Publications Ltd, 66 Portland Place, London W1M 4AD   Tel 0171 580 5533

HMSO Books, Publications Centre, PO Box 276, London SW8 5DT
Tel 0171 873 0011 (enquiries) and 0171 873 9090 (orders)

Books

Building Conservation Directory, Cathedral Communications, 66 Strathleven Road, London SW2 5LB   Tel 0171 738 6462

Buying and Selling Your Home by Martin Village, Piatkus

Conservation Planning, Planning Aid for London, Calvert House, 5 Calvert Avenue, London E2 7JP   Tel 0171 613 4435

Cutting Through The Red Tape, Planning Aid Wales, 4th Floor, Empire House, Mount Stuart Square, Cardiff, CF1 6DN   Tel 01222 485765

Directory of Public Sources of Grants, by John Kemp, English Heritage, Building Twelve, Cherry Hill Estate, Old, Northants, NN6 9QY
Tel 01604 781163

Guide to Building Control in Inner London 1987 by Peter Pitt, Architectural Press

Guide to the Building Regulations 1991 by Lawrence W. Davies, Butterworth-Heinemann

The Housing Design Handbook, the BRE Bookshop, Garston, Watford WD2 7JR

Planning for Householders, Planning Aid for London, Calvert House, 5 Calvert Avenue, London E2 7JP   Tel 0171 613 4435

The Readers' Digest Repair Manual

The Which? Book of Do-It-Yourself, Consumers' Association

Source documents

The Building Act 1984; The Building Regulations 1991; Approved Documents, A–N

all from either your local authority, HMSO or local library

Pamphlets

Age Concern fact sheet for home improvement grants, Astral House, 1268 London Road, London SW16 4ER   Tel 0181 679 8000 Fax 0181 679 6069. For information on help available in Scotland contact Age Concern Scotland, 54A Fountainbridge, Edinburgh EH3 9PT   Tel 0131 228 5656

English Heritage Repair Grants leaflet, English Heritage, Fortress House, 23 Savile Row, London W1X 1AB   Tel 0171 973 3049

Getting The Best From Your Builder, the BEC, 82 New Cavendish Street, London W1M 8AD

House Renovation Grants booklet, from your local council
Office of Fair Trading leaflets, which explain how to complain about unsatisfactory goods and service, from OFT, PO Box 2, Central Way, Feltham, Middlesex, TW14 0TG   Tel 0181 398 3405

Index

garages, security, 132
gas supply, 94, 106, 116
glazing, building regulations, 82
grants, 16-20
groundworks, 101-2
grouting, tiles, 124, 146
guarantees, 49-50, 158, 159-60
gutters, 109, 169

halogen lighting, 128
heating systems, 109-12, 116
  building regulations, 82
  grants, 17
  maintenance, 171
  radiators, 109, 111, 130-1, 149
high court, 164-5
historic buildings, grants, 19, 20
HMO grants, 17
hot water systems, 111

illness, 16, 118-19
incandescent bulbs, 128
inspections, building regulations, 88-9
insulation, 17, 82, 170
insurance:
  architects, 37
  architectural technicians, 43
  builders, 49-50
  project managers, 41
  surveyors, 31
invoices, 155

JCT Minor Works Contract, 59-60
joists, 106, 141, 142

kitchen units, 124, 127
kitchens:
  electricity sockets, 129
  lighting, 128
  planning, 122-5, 133-5
  tiling, 146

Latent Damage Act (1986), 158
lathe and plaster, 106
lavatories, 125, 126, 147
legislation, consumer rights, 156-9
lighting, 127-9
  bathrooms, 127
  kitchens, 125
  security, 132
  switches, 129
lintels, 106
listed buildings, 69-72, 76
loadbearing walls, 106

loans, 14, 159
local authorities:
  building regulations, 78-92, 98-9, 119
  grants, 17-19
  planning permission, 68-78, 98-9, 119
location assessment, 10-11
locks, 132
London Building Acts, 79
London Grants, 19
LPG (Liquefied Petroleum Gas), 109

maintenance, 11, 168-71
materials:
  assessing the builder's work, 139
  delays in supply of, 119
  discounts, 150
  guarantees, 159-60
  paying for, 155
membrane sheets, floors, 143
minor works assistance, 18
mirrors, 129
money *see* finances
mortar, 142
mortgages, 14, 15, 16

natural gas, 109
negotiation, complaints, 161, 162
night storage heaters, 112

oil, heating systems, 109
overdrafts, 14
oversite, 104

painting, 148-9
partition walls, 105
payments *see* finances
pilfering, 150-1
pipes, utilities, 106-7
pipework, external, 109
planning, 5-25
  rooms, 121-35
planning permission, 67-78, 98-9, 119
plaster:
  cracks, 149
  painting, 148
  plastering, 12, 145-6
plasterboard, 142, 144-5
plumbing *see* water supply
Polyfilla, 149
priorities, 12
project managers, 39-41
purlins, 107

quotations, 11-12, 54-5

185